A NEBRASKA FOOTBALL

A WALK ON
GL TO RY

GRAHAM NABITY
BY ARTHUR L. LINDSAY
FOREWORD BY MIKE RILEY

A WALK ON TO GLORY

Cross Training Publishing
15418 Weir Street #177
Omaha, NE 68137
(308) 293-3891

ISBN: 978-1-938254-66-6

This book is manufactured in the United States of America.

A WALK ON . . . TO **GLORY**
God honors those who honor Him

He who speaks on his own does so to gain honor for himself, but he who speaks for the honor of the one who sent him is a man of truth; there is nothing false about him. John 7:18

FOREWORD

When asked to write a foreword for a book that describes competing for the glory of God, I welcomed the opportunity, especially because *A Walk On to Glory* focuses on the life, times and experiences of Graham Nabity, an Elkhorn, Neb., native who walked on and earned three varsity football letters as a Husker.

I had the pleasure to coach Graham for two years, so I can relate to him and understand the lessons he learned after deciding to compete at a collegiate program with both stature and tradition. I made a similar decision when I was a senior in high school in Oregon and attended Alabama.

High school graduates who decide to walk on and shoot for the stars do not do it for their own glory. Most compete for the **glory** of God and the honor that comes with it. As an I-back, fullback and special teams contributor, Graham played in 36 games at Nebraska and earned Academic All-Big Ten honors, a HERO Leadership Award and multiple honors on the Tom Osborne and Brook Berringer Citizenship Teams.

Those achievements are meaningful, but the lessons he learned this past year go well beyond football, and that's why Art Lindsay decided to write a book through the dual lenses of Graham and the Nebraska Fellowship of Christian Athletes.

Both a national and global speaker, Lindsay has written 13 books, including *One Final Pass: The Brook Berringer Story.* His newest book, *A Walk On to Glory,* features the powerful influence that faith delivers during the toughest times.

Graham read scripture at Sam Foltz's memorial service in

Grand Island. He was the only Husker player or coach to speak during the service.

The overall experience from such a monumental tragedy strengthened Graham's knowledge of God in terms of worshipping, giving thanks at the same time his team was mourning and displaying godly character before, during and after every game.

The greatest thing about football is the lessons you learn throughout the journey. You realize that simple faith, trust and hope help you compete for the **glory** of God and, in the process, it becomes both a blessing and an honor.

Mike Riley, Nebraska Head Football Coach

PROLOGUE

A walk on is a familiar designation in every college and university in the United States, not only in football but in various varsity sports. The significant meaning of the term is though you're not good enough for us to recruit you, if you really want to try to make the team we'll give you a chance to prove yourself.

Becoming a successful walk on has been a hope for hundreds of high school football players in the state of Nebraska for more than a hundred years. Throughout the twentieth century the Cornhuskers had a roster of as many as 200 players, loaded with walk ons.* Now the number is limited to about 140 with 88 of them being on scholarship. Some walk ons actually succeed and make a difference for the team, but more than half don't advance in the program and give up. The 2010 season, for example was typical; there were 20 new walk on players and 15 of them quit by the end of the year.

For those who do continue, most do not rise to prominence, but they still get a uniform, a laptop, Adidas gear and enjoy—endure—arduous practices. Though they can eat with the team, they don't get tuition, room or board—the hefty part of the cost of a college education. A few do eventually prove themselves worthy of at least a partial scholarship. Yet most of these aspiring young athletes, in pursuing their dream of football stardom, mount up huge student loan debt.

There are a few remarkable stories elsewhere of determined high school football players who were not recruited by any college or university but proved their talents as a walk on.

Four time Pro Bowler Clay Matthews is a sterling example. Shunned by all the experts, he walked on at USC and after an outstanding college career was drafted in 2009 by the

Green Bay Packers, where he is a nemesis to every opposing offense.

T. J, Ward only started two games in high school, walked on at Oregon, and became a Pro Bowler in the NFL. He was drafted by the Browns in 2010 and then was traded to Denver.

J. J. Watt walked on at the University of Wisconsin as an offensive back and shifted to defense. He was a second -round draft pick of the Texans and became a Defensive Player of the Year in the NFL.

Jordy Nelson was a walk on at Kansas State. Initially a safety, he moved to wide receiver in 2005 and was drafted by Green Bay, where he is a favorite target of Aaron Rodgers.

Jimmy Williams is one notable Nebraska walk on to make it to the pros—in 1982. In fact as an All-American, he was drafted by the Detroit Lions in the first round— 15th overall.

There are lots of lesser stories of glory in football: whether high school, college, or the pros, but glory is only glory until the shine wears off. The praise and adulation doesn't last. Yet, there is a **glory**, a joy that lasts and lasts.

---

*When Bill Callahan came from San Diego to replace Frank Solich as Head Football Coach for the Huskers he was overwhelmed by the number of players on the roster. He said he was used to an NFL roster of 55 and couldn't manage 150. During his four-year tenure he greatly restricted the walk on program, much to the dismay of most alumni and to the chagrin of dozens of aspiring high schoolers who had yet to prove themselves. But a positive thing he brought from the NFL—he instituted a team chaplain program. (Matt Penland was the first chaplain with full access to players and coaches; and he was succeeded by Brett Byford a former offensive center for Nebraska.)

Contents

CHAPTER ONE

From High School Prominence to Walk On Obscurity

I have been crucified with Christ and I no longer live, but Christ lives in me. The life I live in the body, I live by faith in the Son of God, who loved me and gave Himself for me. Galatians 2:20

This is the unique story of a 2012 walk on football player at the University of Nebraska. He was a steady, persistent type of guy, unknown to most in the Husker Nation. He was unheralded, yet he refused to quit in spite of a lack of playing time. This determined young man was certain God could use him as a Cornhusker, though he never gained prominence on the gridiron and had little recognition from the wild-eyed-and-dedicated fan base.

In his first two seasons even some of the most ardent supporters had to check the player roster in the program guide when occasionally #29, Graham Nabity, ran out onto the field.

This kid, who had been a talented high school running back, was obscured by the abilities of scholarship athletes. He carried the football only seven times during his 4½ years as a Cornhusker (redshirting his first year). What he yearned to do was "carry the rock to the end zone." He didn't have a chance, however, to carry the ball even once during his junior year of 2015 or his senior year of 2016. Nonetheless, he worked hard to insert himself into the game any way he could, and consequently his contribution to the Cornhuskers on special teams during kickoffs and punts became significant. More importantly, his spiritual influence among the players—not known to the average fan—gained for him a **glory** that cannot fade.

An interesting sidelight to some games was contributed by Graham's good friend Trevor Reinmatz. He made a cardboard sign, which read when unfolded—We (with a big heart) Graham Nabity. (see picture section) Invariably it was flashed on the stadium jumbo screen.

In recognition of his behind-the-scenes impact on the team and his importance on special teams, he made the travel roster and started for his last three seasons; and Coach Mike Riley put him on scholarship in the spring of his junior year and for all of his senior year.

It's exciting to see how one who was pushed aside as a player could have a significant impact on the team by his insistence on giving **glory** to God in all circumstances. As time went on, Graham's determined stick-to-itiveness to be a loyal Husker and a witness for Christ earned him a respect from all who knew him intimately. "Everything you do on earth will come to an end," Graham told a high school assembly in Central City, on January 11, 2017. "That's what really keeps me going—making God known."

Of course, just like any recruited player, this six-foot, 220-pounds-of-muscle (now trimmed down to 195), I-back had high expectations when he joined the Huskers in 2012. He had an outstanding career at Class B Elkhorn High School after transferring there in his junior year from Millard North. He was voted all-state after gaining 1,532 yards as a running back in his senior year. Those are pretty good credentials for a mere walk on.

When he arrived on campus, Bo Pelini was head coach for the Big Red and Ron Brown was his position coach. In the beginning though, for all practical purposes he was little more than a live tackle dummy, serving on the scout team. He chafed under the term Brown used for them—"green shirts." And, being consigned to the scout team gave him no chance to compete for a position on the second team.

Even so, he practiced diligently, striving to move up the depth chart, but to no avail. He couldn't even enjoy the highly acclaimed "tunnel walk"—the team pouring out onto the field to the wild applause from the tens of thousands in the stands. "It hurt," he said, "to be all hyped up, just to sit on the sidelines."

Then in 2014, after the outstanding Andy Janovich graduated, Graham thought surely his time had come, as he switched to fullback. With the change of coaches, however, his playing chances vanished. He was not on the field, except for special teams on punts and kickoffs, executing 5 tackles, which ranked him as a tackle leader—and making one crucial fumble recovery.

During his last two seasons he wasn't used as a running back even once. So, there was no chance to prove himself in a game. Even so—since kicking is such a big part of football—as a special teams player he was in most games about a third of the time. And as such he was a force to be reckoned with, tackling with vigor and vitality. One such collision in the 2016 Ohio State game, however, was so powerful that he suffered a concussion and had to sit out the Minnesota game the following week.

Yet, thankfully, Graham, when he had come to a lasting faith in Christ as a teenager, realized that there is a greater **glory** to be gained than what comes from an adoring crowd in a football stadium. Besides being a standout player at Elkhorn High School, he was a spiritual force to be reckoned with. He led a Bible study for students every Wednesday morning and had a pre-game prayer with teammates on the field every game day morning. Fifteen to twenty of the Antler players also met together on Friday mornings, where Graham shared a Bible verse each week. Players would then write it with Sharpies on their arms to wear for the game that night.

Continuing in that same spirit, when he got to Nebraska he immediately became involved with the Fellowship of Christian Athletes and wound up serving as the huddle president his last three years. He even spent the summer months between his junior and senior seasons as an intern with the state organization and under the leadership of Coach Brown he eagerly joined in the circle of prayer in the middle of the field after each game (see picture section).

When Brown was let go after Bo Pelini was fired, Graham stepped up to fill the void. "I knew," he said, "that as a student exercising free speech there could be no objection." Robbie Trent, the FCA rep for the Lincoln area encouraged him to do so.

Even more significantly, Head Coach Mike Riley approved of the plan to continue the tradition. Graham led that prayer for the first time after the 2015 Spring Game in Memorial Stadium and then for every game the next two seasons, concluding with the Music City Bowl Game in Nashville, December 30, 2016.

Of course, the purpose of those post-game prayers is not

to make a sanctimonious show. Rather it is a heartfelt desire to give **glory** to God—honoring Him—win or lose. The huddle in the middle of the field might start out with a group of twenty and grow to forty or more as others join in. Often it turns out to be a mixture of players and coaches from both teams, further testifying to a unity in Christ for all who believe. There are no scripted, formal prayers but rather a spontaneous declaration of faith. The praying is not lengthy—players need to get on to other things: showers, family, girls, etc. Be that as it may, Graham and countless others believe it is necessary to praise God regardless of circumstances, even after blowout losses like at Ohio State or Iowa in 2016. Television cameras usually turn away uncomfortably from the scene, but hundreds of fans wait and watch admiringly from the stands, saying, "That's what it's all about!"

In addition to his outward leadership, Graham was also constantly looking for opportunities to encourage his teammates—and others—for Christ. He was avid in making use of social media. His tweeting reached hundreds of people, (Read some of them in chapter seven) including most of the Cornhusker players and coaches.

While not studying or playing football, Graham busied himself with many volunteer opportunities in Lincoln and beyond, such as Uplifting Athletes, People City Mission, Pilger tornado relief, Lincoln Food Bank, Husker Hotline, and with other team members on visits to hospitals and community rec centers. Far from the limelight of such events, he also sought out underprivileged kids in Lincoln, individually taking dozens of them—two or three at a time—under his wing. He took them not only to fun events but especially to youth group meetings at church (which often ended up being their favorite). Occasionally he could scrounge tickets from other players to get kids into Husker games, and from time to time he would load up his car for a trip to his family home in Omaha.

All of this was a special joy, giving of himself, expecting nothing in return. Since a college student is often short on funds, Christ's Place the church he attended while in Lincoln, helped him cover the hefty food costs of feeding hungry kids.

"It was satisfying as a father," David Nabity said, "to see a son more invested in the hearts of others than self-promotion in athletic performance."

During his time at Nebraska he was an example of the true meaning of a UNL STUDENT-athlete who lives his life for something greater than himself or personal goals and accolades. Six times he was on the Nebraska-Scholar-Athlete Honor Roll and was named an Academic All-Big Ten for 2016. Following the 2014 season, he received the HERO Leadership Award honor that is awarded to student-athlete leaders from each varsity sport. He was on the Tom Osborne Citizenship Team for four years—2014-2017, and for three consecutive years he was named to the distinguished Brook Berringer Citizenship Team—2014-16.

CHAPTER TWO

The Boy who almost Wasn't

I know that you can do all things; no plan of yours can be thwarted. . . .The Lord blessed the latter days of Job more than the first. Job 42:1, 12

Kim and David Nabity married young: she was 21 and he was 20. Within a year they were blessed with their first child, a daughter, Amber. Then in rather quick order came Justin and Krystal and Ben. They were very content, and thought their family was complete so they considered a "physical fix" so as not add to their brood. When they consulted their gynecologist, Dr. Tom Dolnicek, however, he urged caution, "Wait at least two years before you make such a decision." They followed his advice, but they were satisfied—their quiver was full.

Before their beautiful second son was two, however, tragedy struck the Nabity household. Kim's parents, Matt and Margerite Holzapfel, convinced Dave and Kim to let them drive the two youngest kids, Ben 2 and Krystal 5, to Sarasota, Florida for a month so that they would have more time to spend with Justin and Amber. Reluctantly the Nabitys agreed, but then felt sick at their stomachs as soon as they did.

Dave even had bad dreams about a catastrophe and considered flying down to Florida to bring the two infants back. Before the month was up, the unthinkable happened. Kim's mother had put Ben in his crib for an afternoon nap. When he woke up, he silently crawled out of the crib, toddled out of the house without anyone seeing him, stumbled into the family swimming pool, and drowned.

The Nabitys were devastated. "I cried so hard my head hurt," Kim recalled even a quarter of a century later. "I just couldn't stop screaming, my anguish was so deep."

For David, he cried so hard, for so long, that he had a constant ringing in his ears from the pressure. "A child has a special place in your heart," he said, "and when he is suddenly gone it leaves an empty hole."

How does a family cope when the bright future they had anticipated is shattered, when darkness sweeps in unexpectedly? What had seemed a perfect life for David and Kim suddenly was gone, threatening to rip them apart. Certainly, had it not been for their faith in Jesus Christ they would have been totally engulfed in despair.

"But, in the midst of the mourning," Dave declared, "the Holy Spirit showed up! I was so grief stricken that all I could do was read the Scriptures and seek God's voice and guidance. He showed me some amazing things during that time that I know were special treats He wanted me to learn to give me hope and to know that He didn't abandon me or my family.

"One such treat was the story of Job. After all Job had gone through, losing everything but his wife, God restored by giving him double of everything he had before. Double of all the wealth and livestock, but God gave Job only one more portion of his kids, not double of his seven sons and three daughters he had before." God showed David there was no need to double the children because they were alive in Heaven with God. That little treat from the Holy Spirit gave Dave and Kim great comfort knowing they will see Benjamin again.

He and Kim were encouraged to trust God for healing from the loss of their son and soon Kim became pregnant. In a dream David had a clear image of an ultrasound—a boy. Yet Kim gave birth to a lovely daughter, Savannah.

She was such a delight to her parents, because she was one who liked to snuggle. "I loved to just rub my hand through her hair while she was sleeping. It was such a joy," David said with delight.

Pain at the loss of Ben was ebbing away.

They continued to work on having more children and Kim became pregnant again. When they both visited the doctor's office to see the ultrasound, the image on the monitor matched the dream Dave had before Savannah was born. God used that dream to show the Nabitys He is in charge, He was guiding their steps, and that when the time was right they would have another son. On May 12, 1993, one day after the birthday of Justin Nabity (Graham's older brother), Graham Roland came kicking into the world.

Not finished yet in pouring out blessings, God graced them with a fourth daughter, Madison, affectionately called "Moo". Kim and Dave were pleased beyond measure—their cup was full and running over.

Graham, however, proved to be more than a handful of action in motion. From his earliest days it was evident he was filled with a full-throated and competitive spirit. "Whether it was checkers or running a race or whatever," David observed, "he wanted to win. He was only seven when he started playing tackle football—as a KWAA Dolphin. His uniform was bigger than he was. I was really angry at the time that the coach played him against nine-year-olds, and he really got knocked around a lot. It was a rough time for Graham."

His parents considered taking him out of the sport until he was a little bigger, but they decided to keep him in and try to encourage him through that first year.

A great source of help came when after the death of Kim's mother as a result of an automobile accident, her 82 year old father, Matthew Holzapfel, came to live with them, taking a room in the basement. "Dad had to work hard and was gone quite a bit to feed and clothe seven of us," Graham observed, "so it was a real blessing to have grandpa around."

Consequently, the octogenarian helped to fill the void and became a close friend to his grandson. He wasn't very mobile, but he would sit on the porch and throw passes to Graham, who would bring the ball back and then run another route. On and on it would go, the eager grandson and the tired old man until grandad's arm would give out. Graham loved every minute of the time with his grandfather. Besides being fun, it served to build confidence in the young boy and give him a lasting comfort with the grip of the football.

When Graham suited up at age seven to play peewee football, his grandfather was ready and eager to go to every practice and of course to every game. One Saturday while the two of them were at home together, watching a Nebraska football game on television, his grandad assured him, "Hey, you're going to be on that screen someday."

The old man and the young boy always focused on sports, when the newspaper arrived, grandad would throw the news section aside, saying, "Who reads that stuff!" And go right to the sports pages.

When he was 90, however, that emphasis turned into a

disaster. "I had the flu one day," Graham recalled, "and my grandpa loving me and serving me as he always did brought up some snacks for me while I was lying in bed. He simply asked if I wanted to read the sports and see when the games were and I of course said yes. He immediately rushed down to get me the paper as fast as he could but slipped down the stairs hitting the back of his head on the step which ended up cracking his head and leaving him in a pool of blood." Graham rushed down and held him in his arms as he watched his grandfather's eyes roll to the back of his head and thought this was the last moment with his grandad.

After a trip to the emergency room and multiple stitches, once again, Grandpa bounced back and regained his normal health. "This was one of many times," said Graham, "that we thought our stout grandfather wasn't going to make it." Shortly thereafter, Matthew had to be moved to an assisted living facility due to further falls and his need to have assistance with walking. To encourage him, Graham said demandingly, "Grandpa, you have to stay alive to watch me play high school football."

Another type of testing—far removed from sports—came to the youthful Graham when his dad decided to run for governor in 2005. Dave had stiff opposition in the Republican primary, even though he first began campaigning for Governor of Nebraska when it was an open seat.

Six months later, the sitting Governor, Mike Johanns was appointed to be Agricultural Secretary under President George W. Bush. That allowed the Lieutenant Governor, Dave Heineman, to move into the Governor's chair, giving him all the advantages of an incumbent. If that weren't enough competition, a year after that, Nebraska's legendary football coach, Tom Osborne, also decided to join the race, putting Dave at a massive disadvantage.

Dave and the family campaigned all over the state of Nebraska, and Graham could be seen roller blading up many of the main streets, handing out goodies during parades. "It took only about three parades to totally burn out the whole family from helping," said David. "Grumpy Graham" let it be known that he'd like to skip that activity. Campaigning was not his thrill. At twelve years of age he didn't fully grasp the gravity of the situation and wanted to stay home and play with his friends.

By the time Dave learned how "low in the polls" he was, it was very close to the debates so he decided to stay in the race to try to influence the policy decisions of the winner. In the end, however, it didn't matter much. The well-oiled political and financial machinery of the Heineman camp won the race—defeating both Nabity and Osborne.

Nonetheless, David garnered great, lasting respect for his integrity and forthrightness, so much so that he is frequently asked to fill in as a host on talk radio station KFAB in Omaha and most recently has hosted a weekly call-in show on Saturday mornings. Dave has become well known as someone who will stand up for Biblical values as well as righteousness in the marketplace and from our elected officials.

The next year, before Graham entered his sophomore year, his dad arranged for him to have one-on-one focused training under the famed former running back for the Cornhuskers, Johnny Rogers. It helped prepare him for the aggressive brand of football played at Millard North High School.

Another factor that helped Graham was running track. His dad suggested he move out of long distance running to sprinting. This was so he would have a better chance of doing well as a running back in football—with quick, short, twisting bursts of speed. It worked! Graham eagerly moved forward in the program at Millard North, but in his sophomore year he developed inflammation in his hip, primarily due to the excessive weight lifting and growing pains. It was painful for Graham even to walk, and much more to play football. The coach, however, was insistent that he be ready to play through the injury.

Along with these trials, Graham realized he wouldn't be used to his full potential in the wish boned triple option styled offense. He and his dad began to look elsewhere for an offense that relied on the running back and not on the quarterback.

"The doctors were telling us that Graham had to quit practicing for a while and allow the inflammation to subside after receiving an injection in his hip. It became pretty clear the coaches were not going to appreciate that," said David. So he and Kim began looking for an opportunity to transfer to another school after Graham had successfully worked through the rehabilitation process with Gibby Duvall.

After months of physical therapy to retrain his "inner core strength," Graham had the opportunity to visit with Coach Mark Wortman at Elkhorn High School about transferring. Both Dave and Graham had watched Elkhorn play Millard South in a playoff game and were very impressed with the offensive scheme Elkhorn ran. "We both felt very good about Graham's chances of excelling under that system," Dave said. When Coach Wortman showed an interest in having Graham transfer, Dave and Kim put their house up for sale, the only house that most of the kids had ever known, because Graham was not allowed to merely "transfer" there. The district rules stated that the family had to actually move and live in the Elkhorn district if he wanted to play there.

The move presented big problems for other members of the family. His sister Madison blamed Graham for the loss of her friends in their former neighborhood and school. It was a difficult transition for her and his other siblings were also heartsick about the "family home" being gone.

Before the move, in the spring of Graham's junior year, he had an unfortunate experience apart from football, because of high school rivalry in Omaha. He and four of his friends had gone for dinner, along with some girls, at a Taco Bell on West Maple Street.

They were enjoying themselves until about forty tough guys from a rival school came in and gathered around them menacingly and their leader had a gun tucked in his belt. Words grew especially heated when one of the girls accused the opposing students of destroying one of her friend's Mustang earlier with a baseball bat. It was known in Omaha that this group went around causing trouble. The guy with the gun said everyone should calm down and go outside.

The girls went their way and Graham and his friends piled into his car—with the intimidating students crowding around it. He didn't want to back up and hit some of them, making matters worse, so he rolled down his window to ask if everything was okay. Without warning, the nearest guy sucker punched Graham in the face, breaking his jaw and leaving him stunned for several seconds. His friend in the passenger's seat shook him back to reality, and he backed up and drove away from the scene. He was so dazed by the blow— that other than spitting up blood—he didn't realize much until the next morning in the hospital with his parents. He had to be on a soft diet for six weeks and lost a lot of weight.

In reflection of the incident Graham said, "A couple of them wound up in jail and most of them are not doing so hot right now."

As Graham became healthier it was time to begin training to get into shape. The summer before beginning his junior season at Elkhorn he worked with Gibby Duval at Explosive Edge to train as college athletes do to increase speed, agility and strength.

That turned out well for Graham because when the fall season came he was ready. Playing every other series, a system Wortman utilizes to keep his players fresh for four quarters, Graham was able to rush for 988 yards and scored 11 touchdowns. The team qualified for the Class-B State Championship game, only to suffer a crushing defeat at the hands of Crete—0-34. The loss was so devastating to Graham that he pledged, "We'll beat them next year."

In areas other than sports, in the early years of his life, Graham had experienced a consistent spiritual example from his parents. They were faithful in their church attendance and dragged their children along, which naturally included Graham. He went of course, but not willingly; he wanted to have fun with his friends or stay home and play video games. "None of it was real in my life," he recalled, "but one night at youth group I 'prayed the prayer' just so I wouldn't go to hell. But it didn't change anything in my life. I would sneak out at night to be with my friends, who always wanted me to drive so they could make a quick escape after sneaking beer out of gas stations. I never drank beer or used drugs, but it was exciting to be with them—until the night we got pulled over due to my friend driving through someone's lawn. The police came and then called our parents. I was sitting on the curb when my mother arrived. I had been bold up to that point, but I broke down when I saw the sadness in my mom's face."

The Nabity family had been searching for a new church home for nearly a year when they first attended Calvary Chapel West Omaha, which met at that time in Kiewit Middle School. They liked what they saw and heard from the pastor, Todd Doxzon.

Todd had been a standout football player at Iowa State— the starting quarterback all four years. He wasn't drafted, but as a free agent he signed a contract with the New York Jets. It was a short-lived career, however, when he pulled a hamstring in camp. He had opportunities with other NFL teams and arena football teams for a few more years, then he finished up his degree at Iowa State. In 2005 he joined the staff of the Fellowship of Christian Athletes as a rep in Omaha, his hometown, where he had been a three-sport athlete at Millard North. After two years with FCA, however, by a step of faith, Todd started the church, which has a specific purpose:

"We exist to equip loving, self-feeding, replicating servants whom God will use to radically change the world."

Graham became enthusiastic about attending church and developed a personal relationship with the pastor, who was a natural magnet for the aspiring young athlete. Graham immediately jumped right into the mix of things, helping with set up on Sunday mornings and attending Wednesday night youth group. He was experiencing a sort-of relationship with Jesus, but he was not fully committed. He was balancing things assuming that everything was okay "As long as I'm not as bad as the next guy." He had no desire for drugs or alcohol, but there was an obstacle in his way.

There was a girl.

Graham's focus was on her continually. She became number one in his life. He could think of little else. It was all about her, and that was not healthy.

Both of them saw it but continued on.

He suffered a crushing loss when she told him that God had told her to break up with him. "I thought the world had been taken from me," he recalled. Although he hit rock bottom, he felt it may have been the best thing that could have happened to him. For the first time in his life, he really had a need for God and got serious about serving Him.

Alone in his room one night praying, lying flat on his back on the floor, repenting, he was suddenly overwhelmed with a peace and confidence that was unexplainable. He experienced the assuring presence of God that was to guide him for years to come. "When I finally put God first, as the Lord of my entire life, it put a fire in my soul to serve God only and helped me become the man I am today. This was the first time in my life that I truly set myself and my desires to the side and put Him first.

"God took hold of me and that began a change in my relationships with others. To those who were believers we held one another in check at school and beyond; if you had failed in some way to be faithful to Christ—anything not of love—you could be challenged to do 10 'accountability pushups' on the spot—in the cafeteria, the hallway, the football field, wherever. We were to be light in the darkness. This was strange to those who did not believe. As a result I was not always invited to their parties." He was learning that it takes a persistency of faith to live a godly style of life in an unbelieving circumstance.

His mother was thrilled with the immediate change she saw in him. "I was really pleased," she said, "when Graham dedicated his life to Christ, because he went from being a self-focused teen to one who was willing to disciple and mentor others in high school. As parents, it gave us a lot of confidence to trust him and know that he wasn't going to do things to get into trouble and that he was hanging with those who were a good influence. Many of the parents of the kids he was influencing were very grateful for his investment in them. It really warmed our hearts."

From that time on Graham was greatly influenced for Christ by Todd Doxzon and grew so extremely close to his family that he wanted to hang out there continually. He felt comfortable enough to show up at dinner time and be welcomed at the table. He wanted to be there to see how they functioned as a family and to be discipled and to grow in his relationship with Christ. He enjoyed that relationship so much that he asked permission of his parents to move in with Todd and his wife Denise for his senior year of high school. (The Doxzon's often would take in kids they had a heart for.)

David was for the plan because he knew the value of having someone outside the family mentoring his son. He reasoned, "Having outside leaders, mentors and spiritual advisers is critical for teenagers and their development. We need more people who are willing to serve in that capacity."

Kim, however, was cool to the idea. She wasn't ready to part with the boy she had nurtured from birth. "When Graham was determined to go and stay with the Doxzon's, because he wanted to be mentored by them" Kim said, "I took it much harder than Dave did. As a mom, I didn't want to let go of my son at such a pivotal time since it was his senior season and our last time to be with him before he went off to college. But on the other hand, I didn't want to stand in the way of what God wanted for Graham. I was willing to put my feelings and emotions aside.

"I was sort of sad because perhaps we were not enough for him. It reminds me of the time Jesus went into the temple and was absent from his parents for three days. I spent a day in prayer and seeking the Scriptures and felt a peace from God to let him go."

Graham's brother and sisters, who knew him most intimately, reveal a true sense of who he was and has become.

SAVANNAH

At the time the family got involved at Calvary Chapel church, Graham's older sister Savannah saw flaws in him. "He became really legalistic and gave me the feeling he was just better than I was 'spiritually.' This affected me, as well as (I thought) the relationship between him and my dad. They were having a tough time getting along, and his church and football were just more important to him at that time." It made me feel as though I was just not 'good enough' to fit his mold for Christians.

"I didn't really relate to Graham during high school and college. I was struggling personally in my walk with the Lord, but recently, in the last two years I have gotten to know my little brother and his heart much more than ever. I was so glad when he was done with football because I felt like I got my baby brother back. Football was draining and a lot of times I could tell it quenched his spirit. After his sophomore year, I knew there was a reason for him to be there. It's hard to understand the bigger picture, but I really saw that when Sam Foltz died. Then I knew he was right where God needed him to be.

"That's really when I saw the change in his life. He was called to something higher, and I was in awe of his obedience. Even though he was promised a lot through the coaches that didn't come to pass he CHOSE to stay and be obedient to the Lord. That is hard when everyone else was saying he should go."

Looking back to a happy experience, Savanah said, "I remember a few years ago, on Mother's Day, Graham, Madison and I were able to sit in my car for two hours and just talk as we watched a storm roll in. Growing up it was the three of us, we would have our days when two of us would gang up and pick on the other one, but we were close. That was the first time since high school (2010) that we just talked and had true transparency. I will never forget that day because now I understand my brother's heart and his purpose.

"I am so blessed to be his big sister. It was rough growing up, but he has set an example that makes me want to run toward Jesus every day. I cannot wait for him to be the uncle of my children because I know he will love them right where they are and show them the true love of Jesus. I admire him, and I think he is incredibly brave."

KRYSTAL

His second oldest sister Krystal, (Lund), who now lives in Kansas City, saw those early years a bit differently. "When Graham was born," she said, "I was eight years old and learning how to become a big helper for my mom with all the siblings. Graham, from the start, was my little buddy and I spent a lot of time looking after him and going on little adventures with him. So, I've always related to him very well. I've found that we have a special brother/sister bond and my fondness for him continues to grow as I watch him become an amazing man.

"As Graham has become closer to Christ, I've seen this amazing maturity and love grow in him—stronger than I ever could have imagined. This happened sometime in high school, at a time he was really learning who he was and the kind of example he wanted to be for others. This happened on and off the field, where he let his leadership and trust in Jesus guide him through every path forward—always pushing himself to not let his personal desires lead the way

"I can't really recall any 'flaws' per se as I think back to his younger years and envision my baby bro—the sweet, little rascal he was as a younger brother. But overall, I feel like Graham experienced the normal growing pains any boy goes through from their childhood, to middle school and into high school—learning to do chores (or not to). Take care of yourself/standard hygiene, learning to explore/ be adventurous and figure out how to be a good son/brother/friend, etc. I think a key difference for him, though, is that he began to excel in his football career at a very young age, so people have always been drawn to him.

"That continued to follow him as he got into college, so something I think he may have constantly struggled with was how to accept the admiration and praise from everyone while maintaining his humbleness. I have had the privilege of watching Graham grow up over the years into the wonderful man he is today. I am so proud of him and want his life to be a showcase for what faith and commitment and trust in Jesus can do for someone. He is a walking example of Jesus, and I'm proud he's my baby bro.

"With how much he has accomplished already, it's crazy to think what else is in store for him, but I know God has a divine plan for him and will continue to use him in ways he can't even think of just yet."

MADISON

Graham's only younger sibling, Madison, saw him as a hot head in middle school and high school. "When we moved out to Elkhorn," she recalled, "we were the new students and everyone wanted to pick on us. They liked to make him mad by talking about his little sister. So he would either snap back with words or almost get into a fight about it."

"Graham and I were the best of friends in elementary school. And I mean best of friends. We were always going on adventures, in the creek when it was hot out or if it was frozen. We would even play in the mud in the creek. No matter what we did we always did it together. On one instance we were walking in a cornfield and I stepped on a piece of wood that had a nail in it, and the nail went through my foot. He came running over, picked me up and carried me home! This is one of my fondest memories, because he was always my protector.

"I remember when he built a treehouse all by himself. He has always been one to strive to accomplish things. When we got to high school we drifted. But now it's nice being able to have my best friend back.

"The one major change I saw in him was when he went through heartbreak in high school. This is what really sent him on the path to where he is now. I say that because he seemed (I could be wrong) kind of lukewarm in the faith, and that relationship was making him that way. After that breakup I think he discovered how great the love God had for him was and what He had in store for him."

JUSTIN

Graham's only living brother was already eleven years of age when he was born. Nonetheless, almost from the time he could walk he wanted to be with his big brother. "Whether that be frog hunting, wading across creeks or searching through the woods," Justin remembers, "he always wanted to be out with me experiencing new things.

"During his formative years I had gone away to college, spent time living in England and Costa Rica, got married, launched a business and then started a family. But I recall that when he was a kid he had a level of selfishness that was concerned about his own interests. He was very persistent about wanting to be doing sports or other activities all the time, asking the rest of us to drop what we were doing in a moment's notice to do it with him and if we didn't comply, he would have a bad attitude toward us. At that time he didn't have a lot of concern for others, pretty typical of most kids.

"Even so, I think we relate to one another well. In a way we are like twins separated by eleven years. We seem to have many of the same interests, desires, faith, strengths and abilities. Anything from sports, competition, adventure, to relationships; we have almost everything in common.

"From a distance, though I had moved away, I saw a change in him when he was finishing up junior high and going into high school. Something happened that turned him on to Jesus, where he began to desire stepping into the gap and being a leader. Most of this was apparent through the way he carried himself in athletics along with church ministry opportunities. This carried over into his years in college which seemed to be the period where he really blossomed. We saw someone who wasn't all about getting attention for himself (like earlier years). Instead he saw it as a way to bless others.

"The whole family saw him lead the high school football team to become champions and we were so proud of him. Then to go to UNL and not continue to rise to athletic prominence; many of us felt like he should have been more selfish and gone after what is more acceptable in today's culture. If you have a gift and can utilize it to elevate yourself, you do it without hesitation. Graham could have gone to many schools with a full ride scholarship and continued to be the leader in the spotlight as he had been at Elkhorn High School.

"In that, he has shown me a level of character that I aspire to have. One in which you surrender to the greater good of others at the cost of losing one of the greatest resources of recognition in our community and be willing to let go of it all for the sake of a purpose that will last for all eternity. For him to be able to endure the sacrifice for what many would say cost him countless doors of opportunity for the future, it inspires me to reflect and question my intentions and desires to make sure they line up with what is God's mission for my life."

Amber

Graham's oldest sister Amber (Stitt) married and moved to Arizona when he was about eleven. That was before a lot of today's technologies, and consequently her connection with the younger kids was only once or twice a year at family times.

"When I would see him," she recalled, "he would always be playful and didn't realize how strong he was. I remember him tackling me often, being a goofball.

"I noticed one summer before he went to college he was always out helping kids; maybe through the church or school. Obviously he has carried this through to college (on the team) and on campus too with other kids he meets and tries to help.

"He is a sweet and good person, and I definitely see his humble leadership from afar, affecting others' lives, and he makes me so proud. Life is busy and we don't catch up much but when we do, I am impressed with his accomplishments at a young age. I am still able to keep tabs on him now through social media or our family group chat. We are always texting all our siblings on a daily basis to keep in touch.

"I didn't really relate to Graham during high school and college. I was struggling personally in my own walk with the Lord; but recently, in the last two years I have gotten to know my little brother and his heart much more than ever. I was so glad when he was done with football because I felt like I got my baby brother back—football was draining, and a lot of times I could tell it quenched his spirit."

As his sister Krystal had observed, Graham did have a

great conclusion, so far as football is concerned, in his senior year at Elkhorn High School. Carrying the ball as many as 25 times a game (playing every other series), he gained 1,532 yards rushing, 300 yards receiving and scored 24 touchdowns. Not only that, but playing both sides of the ball, #29 was just as crushingly decisive against the opposition, tackling with precession and intercepting passes aggressively.

Elkhorn again qualified for the State Championship game and the Antlers would have another chance to face off against Crete. By Graham's senior year his early "football tossing buddy," his grandfather, was in really frail health. He was living in a nursing home and would be brought to the games in a wheelchair by Graham's parents if the weather permitted.

Knowing the aging Matthew couldn't endure the cold stadium seats for the championship game, Dave reached out to businessman Sid Dinsdale of Pinnacle Bank to see if they could use his skybox at Memorial Stadium for that game and the answer was yes. So, on that cold November Saturday in 2011 Matthew Holzapfel had a bird's-eye view to see all the action on the field. During that game grandpa watched Graham score three touchdowns in the second half to win the game and exact sweet revenge against Crete, winning the Class-B Title by a score of 26-17.

To the delight of the whole family, grandpa was wheeled out on to the field to watch up close as Graham received his gold medal. It was an amazing experience for the whole family. Grandpa not only stayed alive to watch Graham play high school football, but he got to see him finish by winning a state championship.

The joy of that moment was short lived, however. Two weeks later, Graham was at a youth group meeting in Belle-

vue when he got a text to come home immediately; grandpa
was dying. Graham sat on the edge of his granddad's bed that
night. Though the old man could not speak, Graham talked
to him calmly about salvation by faith in Jesus Christ. He then
asked him, "Do you want Jesus Christ in your life? Focus on
me." Watching the glow in the eyes of the man he had loved
all of his life, Graham could see, Jesus in his heart, as he led
him through the prayer of salvation.

With that beautiful conclusion of their earthly pilgrimage
together, Matthew Holzapfel departed this life for the next.

It should be noted that Graham's performance during his
senior year had been accomplished by playing just half time
because Coach Wortman followed a plan to flip the offensive
players with each new possession. "Who knew," his dad
observed, "what would have happened if he had played full
time." Even so, Graham was a second-team All-Nebraska pick
by both the Omaha World-Herald and the Lincoln Journal
Star; and was named the honorary captain of the Class B All-
State Team.

Now it was time to give serious consideration to playing
college football.

A Minnow in the Ocean or a Big Fish in the Pond

You did not choose me, but I chose you to go and bear fruit—fruit that will last. Then the Father will give you whatever you ask in my name. John 15:16

It didn't take long after the state championship game for Graham to begin to receive some interest from college coaches to play football. He had visits from several college coaches, including one from Coach Barney Cotton of the University of Nebraska. Barney invited Graham to consider Walking On at Nebraska. In addition to the walk on invitation from UNL, South Dakota State, the University of Nebraska at Kearney, Wayne State and Washburn offered scholarships if Graham attended their school. After visiting South Dakota State and attending the Walk On Presentation at Nebraska he had narrowed it down to two. Graham had a tough decision to make.

South Dakota State was offering a full ride scholarship and their offensive scheme was perfect for Graham. He had a really good visit to the Brookings, SD campus—even had his picture taken in a team uniform. At that time, he was told there were two spots available, and he was one of three candidates. "The first two to accept," he was told, "will get it." His dad encouraged him to grab it: but Graham insisted he had to pray about it first. For years he had been growing in his faith and more than anything he wanted God's will for his life.

His dad appreciated that, but he also wanted his son to go where he was really wanted and loved—to be nurtured by godly coaches.

Dave knew also that the life of a walk on at a big time program like Nebraska could be hard—the university has a vested interest in scholarship players. The facts agreed with his dad; South Dakota State made sense. However, Graham was determined to not rush and wait on the guidance of the Lord before he would make his final decision.

In order to get a more professional opinion on the matter, Dave put in a call to Jim Rose, who for many years had been the official broadcast voice of the Huskers. Still active in radio, Jim knows as much about college sports—especially Nebraska football—as anyone in the state. He was pleased to take the time to talk with Graham. "It depends on what you want from college—football or an education," he said to begin with. "If you go to Brookings you'll be a star because they will give every advantage to a scholarship player, but if you go to Nebraska you will get an education!

"I'm a Big Ten graduate myself and I know the quality behind it. You will never regret your education.

"Nebraska, football will be difficult for you—even if you ever get on the field. As a walk on there will always be 88 scholarship players ahead of you. They will get every chance to excel, every chance to make mistakes—and still get another chance—because the university is invested in them. You will always be swimming upstream, against the normal current.

"Graham, you are a running back and in high school you were pretty good, but I have to tell you that no walk on has started a game for the Cornhuskers since I. M. Hipp in 1978.

"I think you would have a hard time at Nebraska to make an impact, but maybe you can be an influence on the team. The main question is what is God's plan for your life? After four years what will you look back on and appreciate?"

Graham was thankful for the advice but still hadn't heard from God. One of the other athletes had accepted the scholarship offer from SDSU; that meant one more was left for the two athletes to whom it had been offered.

Knowing the seriousness of the timing, Dave asked the counselor at the high school to pull Graham out of class—to discuss and pray about the decision. By the end of the day, Graham had a sense of peace and confidence to call South Dakota State and accept the offer there. While phoning the coach to say "yes" to SDSU, they were calling on another line to tell him that the other athlete, just thirty minutes prior, had accepted the scholarship. So Graham's opportunity at SDSU was gone. That door was shut.

Dave was stunned by the poor timing—to the point of tears. Graham, of course, was also dazed momentarily—who could imagine the value of just thirty minutes? Nonetheless, he was shortly overwhelmed by the peace and confidence he had come to rely on that comes only from God.

Graham notified the coaches at UNL that he was going to walk on. So the die was cast—he would wear the scarlet and cream.

Besides that, there was a plus; he was pleased and excited that his running backs coach at Nebraska would be Ron Brown. Graham knew that from the time Brown first arrived in Lincoln, in 1987 as an assistant to the legendary Tom Osborne, he had been outspoken as to his relationship with Jesus Christ. He also appreciated the fact that Ron led that circle of prayer after each game in the middle of the field with the players and coaches—often from both teams.

Graham's high school career came to a final end in the North-South Shrine Bowl Game on June 2, 2012. On June 4 he enrolled at Nebraska.

"It looked good for him in his redshirt year," his dad remembered, "He was moving up on the depth chart and made the fall camp. Then after his redshirt year, two new recruited running backs came into the program and went to the front of the line ahead of him, without any opportunity to compete for the position. The same scenario was repeated in his second year of eligibility. This didn't look good at all and he and I were both terribly frustrated. I believed the time had come for him to transfer, but I had to leave that decision in his hands."

"It was incredibly difficult," Graham admitted, "to work so hard and still not move up on the coaches' depth chart, wondering why it was another guy and not me." As he and his dad discussed it again and again, his dad was persistent in saying he should transfer so he could play football somewhere else. He, however, was just as consistent, affirming, "It's not about football. It's about the Lord, serving Him wherever He wants me to be."

With that attitude, Graham was in full step with the powerful expression of faith as exemplified by Abraham in Romans 4:20-21: *Yet he did not waver through unbelief regarding the promise of God, but was strengthened in his faith and gave glory to God, being fully persuaded that God had power to do what he had promised.*

His mother's thoughts were opposite to those of his dad. "I know," Kim said, "Dave really wanted him to transfer to

SDSU, but I hated having him caught in the limbo of where he was supposed to be. As a mom, I hated the way Graham continued to get overlooked. It gave me a real heavy heart to see him standing around at the practice when other kids were getting all the reps.

"I always tried to give Graham a positive outlook that his time was coming and that he needed to stick it out; but deep down inside, I was really sad for him. I had big time pride and joy of my son being a part of the Nebraska Cornhuskers, but I just couldn't understand why he wasn't getting more respect. That was a heavy burden for all of us after seeing him excel in high school.

"I'm really proud of Graham for listening only to God's voice and not taking the easy route. Our biggest hope is that his spiritual example will have a lasting impact on his team-mates."

With two years of eligibility left, Dave thought he saw some light at the end of the tunnel for Graham. A change in the coaching staff might at last give his son a chance to shine. He wrote his son an encouraging word, "Perhaps God has allowed this to unfold so you could experience this process to better fashion your character and give you a sense of what it is like to be under these circumstances. That would make sense because you would have always wondered what it would be like had you not experienced this. God has also shown you the value and importance of being involved in various ministries to help you see where the true riches in this life are. In His kindness and because of the love He has for you, there has been a lot of good that has come from you being at Nebraska . . . good that you can build on in many ways.

"I am very impressed with the young man you have become and I sincerely respect you."

Regardless of what might happen with the change in the coaching staff, Graham was devoted to staying at Nebraska! He was firm, in spite of whatever obstacles might come. He was resolute in his goal to pursue **glory** for God in Lincoln.

In his ongoing conversation with his dad, Graham emphasized his own perspective, "It's not about football. It is so much more important than a game." In maintaining that stance, Graham was determined to be not just a hanger-on at Nebraska. In fulfilling the desire of his heart to be an essential part of the team, he constantly looked for opportunities to encourage his teammates for Christ.

One of those was Bo Kitrell, who came as a walk on from Ashland-Greenwood during Graham's sophomore year. "About the first thing he said to me," Bo recalled, "was to invite me to join him for FCA and the Navigators meetings." Bo had become a believer because of godly parents, at the age of four, and he was always ready for growth in his faith.

The two of them became fast friends and, for a time, even roomed together. "He saw God in me," Bo said, "and that was a blessing, but more than that, he challenged me to get out of my comfort zone. Graham was unashamed of the Gospel and was constantly sharing the Good News with others. I too wanted to be as bold." Bo was a second generation Cornhusker; his dad, Barry, had played fullback under Coach Tom Osborne in the 1980s.

Bo, who walked on at Nebraska to be a fullback under Coach Ron Brown, switched to being a tight end in 2017. While maintaining a 3.88 grade point average as a civil engineering major, he is also involved in various ministries at

UNL. He is part of the Leadership Team of the Fellowship of Christian Athletes and loves to lead in worship music.

Another sideline buddy Graham developed a friendship with was Ty Betka, a wide-receiver from Superior, Nebraska. Ty had started his college career at Drake University but transferred back to Nebraska after his redshirt sophomore year.

Ty was the only one who made the team after tryouts that year.

The two became close friends, on and off the field, "Being a light for one another," as Ty described the relationship. Along with Kitrell they all served on the Leadership Team of the Fellowship of Christian Athletes. Much like Graham, Ty had a love for the outdoors and they often went camping together.

Ty had come to faith as a result of attending Camp Kitaki in Omaha as a sixth grader. He had been there before, but that year his counselor was Daniel Ramamoorthy, a freshman at Yale University. They had an instant connection. Daniel, originally from India, had been all over the world and had fascinating stories to tell. And Ty, the small town boy, had lots of questions; he wanted the facts. Daniel was faithful in responding to endless emails for the next two years. Finally, when it was time for his confirmation, in the eighth grade, Ty made his commitment to Jesus Christ. As a surprise for him, his parents arranged for Daniel to fly out for the occasion, and that mentorship continues to this day.

Ty was a political science major at UNL and immediately after graduation joined the staff of Third District Congressman Adrian Smith in Washington, DC. His goal is to make a difference in the world, just as he tried to make a spiritual impact as a member of the Cornhusker football program.

"Bo Kitrell and Ty Betka," Graham said, "were two of a small handful of guys (Lane Hovey, Gabe Rahn, and a few others) on the team that had that walk on to **glory** type of mindset for God. They didn't play football just for personal gain, but for God's gain. They were on a mission daily, whether that was asking challenging questions or pointing to Jesus or just being a consistent light that the men on the team could point to. They would call us 'religious', but we would say 'God fearing followers'. Having them was very helpful to continue to fight the good fight and have a team within the team (God's team) to serve our brothers."

Graham's long-time friend and confidant, Todd Doxzon, pastor of Calvary Church in Omaha, encouraged him with similar words he had from his dad, "To be truly honest with you regardless of playing time, you're going to learn a lot of lessons behind the scene as opposed to being a star."

"It's easy to be a stud and the starter and have all the limelight and score all the touchdowns, but I think the route you have taken will pay huge dividends in the future."

Sure enough, as anticipated, there was a total replacement of the coaching staff at the end of the 2014 season. Graham and other players were pleased at the opportunity to meet Coach Mike Riley and the assistants he brought with him. During the ensuing spring training camp the coaches spoke highly of Graham to the press, and he was hopeful. In the spring game, however, he didn't get to play until the second half and it broke his heart. Then, before fall camp, when two new recruited freshmen arrived on campus he, once again, was pushed to the end of the line.

After the bowl game that December, because Graham got tonsillitis a couple of times a year his parents scheduled a tonsillectomy. Since there was a three week break before the start of winter training, this would give plenty of time for healing. A couple of days after the surgery, however, he began spitting up blood. "So much so," he said, "that I was filling a trash bag."

"I was really concerned," his dad said, "because a neighbor up the street had died from something similar and I knew how risky it was, so we rushed him to Methodist Women's Hospital that was close to our home. We were told to go there in case of emergencies, but they couldn't help Graham so we had to pack up and head for the original hospital. There, after spending hours in the ER and securing an ENT specialist, Graham had his initial surgical incisions recauterized to stop the bleeding."

His mother watched anxiously. "I was pretty focused on just getting him to the hospital and making sure he saw the right doctors to correct the problem," she said. "I thought 'if we could just get him the care in an emergency room they could stop the problem of the bleeding'. But every time Graham would lean back, his oxygen levels would drop; and after pressing the doctors about it, they decided to trim his uvula as well as recauterizing his tonsils. He was having a hard time breathing because of the uvula blocking his airway. Once we got him back to the hospital, my fears subsided."

"It was a grueling day," Graham remembers. "I was all pale until the next morning. In just three weeks I lost 30 pounds, dropping from 210 to 180—I hadn't weighed so little since going into my sophomore year of high school. That threw my recovery time back a couple of weeks.

"I was a week late getting into winter training," Graham said, "and still had my body compensation testing done;

which is done before and after training sessions to see how we do and what kind of gains we get. Needless to say, I was at the top of the list with 20 pounds of lean muscle gained at the end of winter conditioning and spring ball. Shortly after that I was making a switch to fullback and the coaches wanted me to gain another ten pounds. To achieve the 220 pound level I had to consume 6,000 calories a day—which I did."

He didn't achieve his goal of playing fullback, but that added weight made him a nemesis to the opposition as he went barreling down the field on special teams.

CHAPTER FOUR

Circumstance Free

And whatever you do, whether in deed or word, do it all in the name of the Lord Jesus, giving thanks to God the Father through Him. Colossians 3:17

Graham first arrived on the Lincoln campus early in the summer of 2012 to prepare himself physically for the start of fall camp in August. One of the first people he met was Robbie Trent, the Lincoln Area Rep for the Fellowship of Christian Athletes. Coach Ron Brown, who was to be Graham's running backs coach, had advised Trent that this outstanding young believer was coming and they should get acquainted early. For their first meeting (and there would be many more) they met at the Runza Restaurant in the Student Union Building. Besides getting acquainted, Robbie, who is usually quick to get to the heart of the matter, plunged into a brief discussion of the disconnection between the "cultural Christian" mentality and the study of God's Word. He always points out that achievement does not depend solely on man's effort, but on the grace that comes from God. Of course, Graham was in tune with that and immediately got involved with the FCA Monday night Bible study for students as well as the Wednesday noon meeting for athletes at the Training Table.

He and Trent formed a solid relationship and when Graham became a member of the FCA Leadership Team (and eventually the huddle president) he was a valuable sounding board for Robbie in regard to the spiritual pulse of the football team. "He truly was my go to guy," Trent reflected.

Together, Trent and Graham studied *Playing Sports God's Way*. That book, written by Wes Neal, points out that athletic glory is a fleeting fancy, but competing for God's **glory** has a lasting significance. Trent defines the concept this way, "Responding to the Gospel with repentance of sin and belief in Jesus Christ, leading to the worship of God with attitude and effort in the midst of training and competition."

That is exactly where Graham had his focus from the time he first came to faith in Christ when he was in high school. Above all, he wanted to please God; to give God the **glory**. That attitude naturally is easiest when everything is going in your favor, but when your hopes are dashed to the ground it can become more difficult, testing your will to persevere.

During one of his most trying times in his career as a Cornhusker, his dad wrote him words of encouragement of playing free from circumstances: "God wants you to finally resolve to not look at your circumstances, the talent of other athletes, the inconsistencies of coaches, the favoritism and even the idol worship of Husker fans. He wants you to *focus soley on Him on every play, every drill and every success or failure.*"

The Fellowship of Christian Athletes defines it this way: "Stewardship of sports is extracting and doing sports God's way versus man's way. This is done by training athletes, coaches, and all whom they influence how to manage, advance and possess all of the world's athletic activity for the kingdom of God with the goal of seeing every person redeemed by Jesus Christ and conforming to His image."

Ron Brown, who had been Graham's position coach and now is Assistant Head Coach at Liberty University, considers it as simple math, "Doing Sports God's Way = Unbroken fellowship with Jesus Christ while I'm engaged in my sports activity."

Or, in fewer words, Gordon Thiessen, Nebraska FCA staff member, is even more concise, "Competing or coaching for the **glory** of God."

Though not addressing the particular issue, Dave Nabity was right on target when he sent encouraging words to his son. "What matters most is your attitude and focus. I say attitude because everyone makes mistakes, but the one with the right attitude does not allow themselves to get beat down and listen to the lies of the enemy and get defeated.

"I say focus because if your eyes are on Jesus, it is much easier to recover from frustrating plays and disappointments and go right back and attack the opposition."

Adrian Rogers, renowned Baptist pastor and radio preacher, who founded Love Worth Finding Ministries, summed it up as a dichotomy. "Worry looks at God through circumstances. Peace looks at circumstances through God." In other words, worry is self-focused; to be worry-free your focus must be on God.

The great missionary/evangelist of the Twentieth Century, E. Stanley Jones stated the warning succinctly. "Whatever gets your attention gets you!" Or, simply, as the Apostle Paul admonished in Romans 6:16, *Don't you know that when you offer yourselves to someone to obey him as slaves, you are slaves to the one whom you obey—whether you are slaves to sin, which leads to death or to obedience, which leads to righteousness.*

We all make choices.

Brian Conklin, in expanding the term to include everyone, said, "Circumstance free living is living under the authority of God's Word, by God's design, for God's **glory** no matter what your surrounding circumstances might be." Conklin is currently the Fellowship of Christian Athletes head man for Omaha, who during his senior year as a forward for the Nebraska Cornhuskers was the number one three-point shooter throughout collegiate basketball.

Andrew Drevo, who was a teammate with Conklin at Nebraska who then played pro ball in Europe for nine seasons, is also now with the FCA as the Director for the Southeast corner of the state. His take on Circumstance Free is much broader. "When faced with difficult circumstances in life, the follower of Christ can rest in the fact that God is both all-loving and all-powerful. Nothing that happens in life is by accident! There's tremendous freedom in knowing anything and everything that happens in life is, ultimately, for our good and for His **glory**!

"When we look at the life, death, and resurrection of Christ, we see the perfect example of a man who was laser-focused on His mission and purpose and who didn't let pain and fear distract Him. He trusted the Father's will for His life! Like Paul said to the Corinthian Church (1 Corinthians 15:58): *Be steadfast, unmovable, always abounding in the work of the Lord, knowing that your labor in the Lord is not in vain.*"

Daniel Bruce, who played center field for the Nebraska Cornhuskers when they advanced to the College World Series in 2005, is now an attorney in Omaha and keeps active in baseball as a volunteer coach. According to him, "Circumstance free is a learned disposition (through knowledge and practice) to act according to true convictions without fear of potential outcomes. It is rooted and grounded in faith and love in Jesus Christ, trusting in His Sovereignty and Grace. That leads to acting with 'joyful confidence' without 'despair or frustration' about any results. Always remember the promise of Philippians 4:13, *I can do everything through him who gives me strength."*

Whatever the definition, Graham was into it body, mind, and soul.

Of course no one can begin to do anything God's way, whether as an athlete, bricklayer, farmer, or ditch digger without first coming into relationship with God. This is so essential in the walk of life that God has kept it simple enough for even a child to understand:

God has a plan for the world He created and the man He put there to maintain it in Him—John 3:16: *For God so loved the world that he gave his one and only Son, that whoever believes in Him shall not perish but have eternal life.*

Mankind, however, has a huge problem that keeps any man, woman, or child from forming a relationship with God—Romans 3:23: *for all have sinned and fall short of the **glory** of God.*

So, to solve that problem God has provided a free solution—Romans 6:23: *For the wages of sin is death, but the gift of God is eternal life in Christ Jesus our Lord.*

Acceptance of that free gift is necessary and specific—Romans 10:9: *That if you confess with your mouth, Jesus is Lord, and believe in your heart that God raised him from the dead, you will be saved.*

God stands behind this assurance with the rock solid promise of I John 1:9: *If we confess our sins, he is faithful and just and will for-give us our sins and purify us from all unrighteousness.*

That is the perspective of Nate Lewis, the FCA Area Director for South Central Nebraska. He says, "Circumstance free starts with our identity in Christ. When our highest aim is to please Him it frees us from the expectations of the world and gives us purpose to compete for His **glory.**"

Once a person has come into a personal relationship with God through Jesus Christ, he or she can begin to rely on Him for leadership. Graham understood the freedom resulting from such a connection and was in full agreement with Neale's assertion, "The perfect athletic performance is not one in which you try to duplicate the performance of Jesus Christ. It is one in which **you perform like Him because He is performing through you!** It is a supernatural life. The Christian life is doomed to frustration when we try to live it by our own power."

Nowhere in the Bible does God ever promise to change our circumstances! What He does promise, to those who follow Him, is to give them an internal strength to live <u>above</u> the circumstances. Jesus set the example for everyone to take to heart—there is no **glory** without suffering. And His suffer-ing—unlike anything we might have to endure—was as the sinless, innocent Lamb of God!

So as to not be controlled by circumstances—and be cir-cumstance free—Graham and others like him give control of their lives over to the power and authority of the Holy Spirit. Only then does the instruction and assurance of Philippians 4:6-7 make sense: *Do not be anxious about anything, but in every-thing, by prayer and petition, with thanksgiving, present your requests to God. And the peace of God, which transcends all under-standing, will guard your hearts and your minds in Christ Jesus.*

It was with that inner power that Graham was able to bring **praise** to God while *not* being heralded as the key man in Nebraska's running game.

What makes this young man—and others like him—exceptional is that he recognized a third dimension to athletics is essential for a child of God. Hundreds of thousands of athletes around the world perform outstanding feats because they devote their bodies and minds totally to being as perfect as possible. But, when adversity comes they are apt to crumble before your very eyes. It is a third, unseen, spiritual dimension that makes all the difference as it transforms selfish ambitions into positive, God-fearing attitudes.

In his book, Neal suggests a prayer of commitment. "Lord, I realize I have been in control of my athletic ability. Right now, I give to You the complete control of the members of my body, including all of my athletic abilities. They are Yours. I commit them to be weapons for Your use. Amen!"

By enjoying that kind of relationship with Jesus, Graham understood also that his very attitudes were under control—making them pure for the **glory** of God. That transformation of attitude—from self to God—became this young athlete's foundation for perseverance under the strain of trying to move up in the roster of players.

He took Jesus as his role model as it is expressed in Hebrews 12:2-3: *Let us fix our eyes on Jesus, the author and perfecter of our faith, who for the **joy** set before him endured the cross, scorning its shame, and sat down at the right hand of the throne of God. Consider him who endured such opposition from sinful men, so that you will not grow weary and lose heart.*

Graham became determined to experience *joy* in spite of circumstances because the joy from personal recognition is as fleeting as the praise of fickle fans. Jesus exemplified this perfectly. He never sought glory for Himself, but gave all **glory** to His Father.

So, Graham learned to trust God the way Jesus did, knowing God's best was better than anything he could possibly plan. To be "circumstance free" he acknowledged the assurance of Romans 8:28: *And we know that in all things God works for the good of those who love him, who have been called according to his purpose.*

He knew he could never lose if he gave his all for Jesus in each and every situation. That kind of man (or woman) is always a winner in God's eyes. His goal then was to perform for an audience of ONE, not for the praise of the multitudes. In that way even a defeat becomes an amazing learning experience.

During his years as a Cornhusker, Graham's intensity to please God and bring Him **glory** continued to grow. It ceased to bother him that his name was not on the list of starters on the team bulletin board. He was strengthened with a resolve to totally release all his energies to accomplish God's purpose for himself—and equally important—for others. Certainly, it is not to say that was easy. It requires a consistent, close walk with Jesus to gain and maintain such a divine perspective.

Wes Neal also proposed a Christian Athlete's Commitment (to which Graham adhered): "In every athletic situation whether practice or actual competition, I will dedicate myself to give a total release of all that I am—mentally, emotionally and physically—to become just like Jesus. I will determine to conduct myself in a way that will please the Lord rather than gain any recognition from men."

To achieve such a goal, Jesus gave his disciples only one motivational factor—love. Not only did Jesus teach it; He lived it; He showed it—love. The love Jesus demonstrated is not the get-get of the world, but the give-give of God. It is an expression of affection that brings out the best qualities of any individual. It is also what allows an athlete like Graham to participate and be "circumstance free" because the love of God is not like a faucet you turn off and on. It is a constant flow, coming through the presence of the Holy Spirit. In fact, in Galatians 5:22, love is listed as the first fruit of the Spirit.

More importantly perhaps, for Graham and other athletes in a culture that is intent on praise and hero worship, the love of God turns attention away from the individual with a focus on others to give **glory** to God. It normally isn't taken into account, but consider what a football game would be like if it were played with I Corinthians chapter 13—love—in mind. That might just produce an athletic performance *par excellence* without paying attention to the varying circumstances.

An area in which Graham excelled while at Nebraska was learning to be a teammate. As previously observed, it was difficult to see others advance in the lineup when that was what he wanted so much. Nonetheless, he remained constant in encouraging other players. He was determined to be a servant leader. His words and actions were consistent with the Gospel he declared. His tweets, as recorded in chapter seven and read by players and coaches alike, were full of both encouragement and challenge. He did not allow past disappointments to rob him of the joy of the present. Was this easy?

No!

But he persisted. Focus requires total attention. He did not waver from his pursuit of Jesus, which served to deepen his trust in God's will for his life.

While others saw waste, Graham saw purpose and was strengthened by Paul's attitude in Romans 5:1-5: *Therefore, since we have been justified through faith, we have peace with God through our Lord Jesus Christ, through whom we have gained access by faith into this grace in which we now stand. And we rejoice in the hope of the* **glory** *of God. Not only so, but we also rejoice in our sufferings, because we know that suffering produces perseverance, perseverance, character; and character hope. And hope does not disappoint us, because God has poured out His love into our heart by the Holy Spirit, whom He has given us.*

Amber holding Graham
at one week old.

Graham and Dave getting
ready to go for a ride.

Graham's gone fishing
Milford Lake.

Graham's first Tae Kwon
Do match, age 5.

Graham and his cool brother Justin.

Suburban Baseball League. Graham is top right.

Graham's ninth birthday present.

Graham playing on the
Mini Pee Wee team. 2002

Kick Off Tour for Dave's Governor Race: Walt, Marjorie, Krystal, Madison,
Justin, Savannah, Amber, Graham, Kim, Dave. May 2004.

Graham at the Calvary Chapel
Surf Camp in Florida.

Graham running the ball
against Gretna.

Graham's uniform with
Scripture taped to it.

Signing Day celebration with
Pastor Todd Doxzon.

Grandpa Toots and Graham.
November 2011 State Championship game.

Dave, Graham and Kim.

Nebraska team photo of Graham.

First official football banquet. Graham, Tom Osborne, Kim and Nancy Osborne. December 2012.

Luke Gifford, Bo Kitrell, Lane Hovey, Graham Nabity and Ty Betka. Husker and FCA teammates prior to speaking at the York FCA Huddle.

Praying with position coach Ron Brown after the South Dakota State game.

Graham leading the postgame prayer.

Fan Day with nephew
Will and niece Evalyn.

Graham and kids from
The Bay skateboarding facility.

Madison, Graham, Savannah, Krystal, Justin and Amber. May 2013.

Nebraska spring game, 2013.

Graham with children from the
South Africa Resliency Project.

Graham's first African mission trip
with the NU team chaplain Brett Byford, "Bama."

Graham's Indian Reservation
Mission Trip, Yakima, WA. May 2014.

Graham donates to "Locks of Love!"
His sister Savannah does the honors
cutting them off.

Graham playing against Southern Mississippi, 2014.

Football team visitation, Thanksgiving 2015

Graham and Chris Weber
earning their letter jackets,.

Graham having fun in the sun.

Krystal Lund (sister), Graham and
Andrew Lund (brother-in-law).

Graham's friend, Trevor Reimnitz
holding sign at football games.

Fan Day with Mary Campbell, one of Graham's friends from Elkhorn High.

Graham and Allison on a pedicure date.

At the 2015 Hero's Game,
Kim holding Graham's sign.

Graham and Danny Woodhead—
before his locks were cut off.

Kim and Allison at the Iowa game.

Home game prayer before the game.
Nicolette Netz and Graham.

Graham and Allison wedding day.

Graham and Allison on the sidelines.

Foster Farm's Bowl Champions – 2015 Austin Rose, Devine Ozgbo, Andy Janovich, Imani Cross, Harrison Jordan, Jordan Nelson, Graham, Terrel Newby.

Football banquet picture honoring Sam Foltz, 2016. Graham, Branden Reilly, Jordan Nelson, Ryker Fyfe, Spencer Lindsay, Mitch McCann, Nate Gerry, Tanner Zlab.

Kim's favorite picture of Graham in uniform.

An Audience of One

*Jesus answered," I am the way and the truth and the life. No one comes to the Father except through me."*John 14:6

Surely nothing in all of Scripture attests to the authority and sovereignty of Christ than what He said in the verse above. It was an audacious statement! But is it true? If it is true, it gives a guideline for life, and the wise will follow Him all the way into eternity.

As we saw in the previous chapter, man in his natural state, looks at and often dreads circumstances for one reason or another. However, when transformed by the power of Christ, men like Graham look for how God can achieve His purpose in spite of uncertain factors. Often in the gloom of a debilitating moment God is already setting the stage for a spectacular display of His **glory**.

Perhaps the best way to explain what it means—to play circumstance free—is to hear from one who has lived it, from Graham himself. "It means an audience of one! It means the opposite of circumstance-based. Circumstance-based is when you are still operating in the previous play. You are operating on the outcomes before and whether they were good or bad will dictate how well you will play. The problem with that is you limit your potential. It's like choosing to chain yourself up mentally, which doesn't allow you to make the right read and decisions. In sports you can't dwell in the outcome of previous plays. You won't be fully present on the next play and before you know it you are not playing like yourself. Sooner or later you will be off the field.

"The motive of playing circumstance-based will also leave you in such a negative state of mind that after the playing doesn't go well, before you know it you will be stuck in a funk. This negative attitude will carry over to all other areas of your life and will leave you chained up. It has happened to me. I have become such a nasty person at times because of my competitiveness and when things don't go my way.

"Circumstance free is quite the opposite; like the phrase you are truly free. Every single play you have maximum potential to be the best you can be on the field. When bad plays happen they don't control you. You get back up, shake off the dust and thank the Lord for another opportunity, and playing with a type of thankfulness and love that allows you to crush the next play.

An audience of one, A-1, breaks those chains. On every play, in every circumstance, no matter what, you play to your full potential. Audience of One refers to the fact that God is your ultimate audience and He is always there! Whether it's the Saturday mornings in the off season when you are working on your drills and mechanics with no one around, or it's a Saturday night game in Memorial Stadium with ninety-thousand in attendance and the whole state watching on TV. You play the same. No bad play, nothing, can step in the way of you playing your absolute best.

"Audience of One brings about a certain type of confidence. Not worldly confidence in which you depend on your-self, but a spiritual confidence. I like to call it Godfidence. Your identity is in God alone. He loves you in your worst moments and the best. The outcome doesn't matter.

"Audience of One means you always continue to play as unto Him, giving it your all, using your sport and talent as a type of worship to Him. Every time you step on that field you have an opportunity to worship the Creator.

"Whether coaches are watching or not does not depend on how hard you will try to perform your best. These circum-stances should not dictate how well you perform. How hard you try. Our attitude is the only thing we can control in this world. I can't control the lineman in front of me to do his block perfectly, or guarantee that the fullback misses his guy, who just knocks me clean before I could receive the handoff. So much gets thrown at you that you can't control, but you can control your attitude.

"Choosing to be circumstance free will maximize your full potential! Now, who wouldn't want that? It doesn't matter where you are in life, whether at work or school or sport. This can apply in all areas of life. Everything you do you can do as unto the Lord. He is always there. The next opportunity you have, I hope and pray you make the decision to be free to be the person God intended you to be. Now go on out to the world, walk, no RUN! In Godfidence and don't forget your A1 sauce."

Incredibly, that advice comes from a Nebraska Corn-husker who endured one disappointment after another. He never started a game as a running back but had to watch from the sidelines as others accomplished what he longed to do. Nevertheless, he did not wallow in self-pity allowing circumstances to determine who he was. He learned, by God's grace, how to live above the fluctuating conditions of the moment. He yearned to be God's man, to achieve **glory** for his Maker, not himself.

When you fully understand that there is only one person you must please—and to Whom you also are accountable— you suddenly experience an inner freedom to do and to be what He intends, and you can declare with the Apostle Paul, *But thanks be to God. He gives us the victory through our Lord Jesus Christ.* 1 Corinthians 15:57.

Glory Out of Tragedy

For the earth will be filled with the knowledge of the glory of the Lord, as the waters cover the sea. Habakkuk 2:14

Along with Graham in 2012, another walk on addition to the Cornhusker roster was Sam Foltz, a standout football product of Grand Island High School. Since both redshirted their freshman year, they began to form a firm friendship. Sam joined the team as a receiver but quickly focused on punting and became the fourth best in Nebraska's long history.

Since Sam had a major in agronomy and Graham was in construction management, they shared no academic classes together, but they were one in spirit. When #29 took over the after game prayer time in their junior year you could always see #27 nearby. They were as close in relationship as brothers in Christ as their jersey numbers reflected. Sam had a very important spiritual experience early in his life as a junior high school student. Coach Brad Williams had organized an assembly of junior high and high school students in Greely, Nebraska, Sam's hometown in 2005. Coach Ron Brown, who at that time was the Nebraska State Director for the Fellowship of Christian Athletes, was the main speaker. At the conclusion of his message, Ron challenged students to come forward in dedication to Jesus Christ. Sam was one of the dozens who responded and began to walk in faith.

He stayed true to that commitment as indicated by his twitter account hashtag—"Follower of Jesus! Slaying Limits! Nebraska Football #27 Dream Big, Work Hard, Stay Humble." Sam, besides working diligently to be the best kicker he could be for Nebraska, also maintained a high profile as to his faith in Christ. He was highly respected by all who knew him and adored by the widespread Cornhusker fan base. He was all set to play his final year of eligibility as a grad-assistant at Nebraska, and undoubtedly would have been drafted to the next level. Things looked good for both Sam and the Nebraska football program heading into the 2016 season.

No one in Husker Nation was ready for the tragic news of July 24, 2016. Sam and Mike Saddler of Michigan State, along with Colby Delahoussaye of LSU, had served as advisers at a kicking camp for high school players in Wisconsin. Before leaving the camp Sam had shared with the young students the story of his personal, inspiring walk of faith.

A violent storm had swept across the state that day and the roads were wet when the three men headed south late that night. Saddler was driving when he hit a slick spot, skidded, and slammed into a tree. Both Foltz and Saddler were pronounced dead at the scene; Delahoussaye survived.

The following day, the unwanted, unbelievable news of death swept across the Lincoln campus like a raging wildfire. Many members of the football team were in town gearing up for the fall camp, but Coach Mike Riley was out of town. Graham and others sent out word on the internet to gather together outside the Osborne Complex for a time of praise and worship to comfort one another and to honor Sam. In commemoration, someone laid a bouquet of white roses at the foot of the Brook Berringer statue—a former hero of the Cornhuskers, who also had died in the prime of life. A current member of the team, Kieron Williams (junior safety at the time) and Graham hurriedly copied off the lyrics of praise songs, and Graham then accompanied the singing on his guitar. Several hundred joined the spontaneous crowd: team members, other student athletes, and fans.

It was a solemn gathering of reverence and remembrance. They embraced one another in prayer huddles of a half-dozen-or-so, giving silent comfort to one another at a time when words were inadequate.

In the days that followed, Graham and a few other teammates stepped up to hold the team together spiritually, encouraging those who were distraught because of the sudden loss of a friend and colleague.

At the funeral six days later, Graham was asked to read the Scripture passage Sam's mother Jill had selected.

The Cornhusker team continued to honor Sam throughout the fall campaign, proudly displaying his #27 jersey at every game. Movingly, other teams throughout the season-long schedule did the same thing. The most striking tribute of all, however, was at the first game of the season when the Huskers faced a fourth down situation against Fresno State. Coach Mike Riley purposely sent only 10 players of the kicking team out onto the field—minus the punter. The officials instantly threw a flag for the obvious violation. Fresno State, realizing the situation, refused the penalty.

The fans went wild in a standing ovation.

Sam's parents faithfully attended every game of what

undoubtedly would have been an outstanding season for their son. The "Foltz factor" was a strong unifying factor for the team and a reminder for all that we are only on earth for a short pilgrimage.

Facing what comes next is of eternal importance.

Above all, throughout this total experience God received the **glory.** Not only did those who gathered to honor Sam the day after his death hear the Gospel, but more than 140,000 have watched the video on the internet.

CHAPTER SEVEN

Social Media Harnessed for Glory

*May the God of peace, who through the blood of the eternal covenant brought back from the dead our Lord Jesus, that good Shepherd of the sheep, equip you with everything good for doing his will, and may he work in us what is pleasing to him, through Jesus Christ, to whom be **glory** for ever and ever. Amen.*
Hebrews 13:20-21

Although much of what goes on in social media is negative and argumentative, Graham Nabity saw in it the positive value of freely expressing his faith in Jesus Christ. So, while he was still in high school he opened his twitter account in February 2011 with the personal hashtag—*Do you know my Savior yet? Romans 1:16 — [I am not ashamed of the gospel, because it is the power of God for the salvation of everyone who believes: first for the Jew, then for the Gentile.]*

By the time he arrived on the UNL campus in 2012 he was already in full throttle of using it to give utterance to his faith and urging others to follow suit. Yes, he also tweeted about football and his love of the outdoors and of animals, expressing a lot of fun in doing so, but ninety-five percent of the time his almost daily tweeting was used to challenge others—and himself—to live for Jesus. Now he has nearly 1,300 followers. In addition, he has nearly 5,000 friends on Facebook and 2,000 on Instagram.

Graham also had a great deal of enjoyment in posting videos on YouTube. These included a time when he was snorkeling among the fish in the Pacific Ocean, just off of La Jolla, California, climbing the Incline with buddies in the mountains above Colorado Springs, and skateboarding (long-boarding) with his young, underprivileged friends in Lincoln. He also produced two artistic videos, in which he used the dancing talent of Nicolet Netz, a member of the University's dance team, who was a friend of his girlfriend, Allison.

His more significant impact, however, was in his tweeting. On the following pages are samples from more than three years of pithy spiritual expressions from this young athlete. They burst with a desire to give **glory** to his Savior, revealing that Graham has a clear, solid understanding of what a personal relationship with Jesus Christ entails. Most importantly, that came about only by his faith in the grace of God as expressed in Jesus Christ. It is obvious, in reading through all of this, that he didn't learn it from any man. It is a direct gift of God through His Spirit—a moment-by-moment affinity.

11-5-13—Follow faith over feelings. The heart will deceive; God will not.

11-5-13—The devil fears your heart becoming fully free. He knows what can happen. What are you waiting for? If he knows, shouldn't you? Go to God. BE FREE.

11-7-13—Love like Jesus.

11-9-13—It's time to break that Michigan streak.

11-12-13—Whatever you feed will lead. Choose life.

11-13-13—Why follow the created when you can follow the Creator.

11-15-13—I'm leaning my emotion on God.

11-15-13—Great things come with time. Keep fighting.

11-16-13—It's time to run at these guys like David with Goliath. Ain't nobody invincible.

11-19-13—Ever thought of a world without fear and guilt? Well, there is such a thing. His name is JESUS! Be free, you were created for this.

11-19-13—How bad do you have to hate somebody not to tell them about Christ and what's at stake, heaven or hell. Remove your fear of men. Be on mission.

11-23-13—The thing about playing for an audience of 1 is that there is no difference in playing for a title or not. Either way we're giving it our all.

11-23-13—The only thing that matters in this stadium that holds over 1-hundred-thousand is the 1.

11-27-13—Having trouble finding things to be thankful for? Got two working legs? You're blessed.

12-5-13—It's a new day. A new page. How will you write it?

12-9-13—Just come home.
He loves you,
You were meant for this.

12-15-13—My two homies gave their lives to Christ today.
Amazing what God can do in just two days.

12-15-13—God, you are all I need.
Thank you.

12-16-13—No day is given
That's why we call it the present.
Spend time with Jesus
You never know when it's your last.

12-25-13—Now faith is being sure of what we hope for and
certain of what we do not see Hebrews 11:1. How have you
shown faith today?

1-3-14—So you say you love GOD, RIGHT??
How have you spent time with Him today?

1-13-14—Who are you trusting to pay the penalty of your
sins?
Your good works can't save you.
Trust God. Be saved.

1-15-14—It's the times we are running low on God's joy that
we fall into temptation. He is there. Be filled. Be joy.

1-15-14—Purity, the most peace receiving action.
I dare you to try it!

1-16-14—God, I don't want to say anything but thank you.

1-17-14—God is enough!

1-19-14—Had a blast serving the homeless with food and shoes with the Skate for Cancer crew.

1-20-14—Single? Feeling lonely? You don't have to be. Take your loneliness up to God and BE FILLED.

1-21-14—God would rather die than live to have you.
Remember that.
He loves you.

1-22-14—King Jesus gave me everything on that tree. So you best know I be giving Him everything.

1-23-14—More money can't buy you more time. Spend your time on things that last. Make a difference today.

1-30-14—I may be weak
But your Spirit is Strong in me.

1-31-14—You are either making moves or making excuses.

1-31-14—LADIES,
God didn't make you like anybody else.
Don't let nobody tell you that you're anything less,
Cause You are Beautiful!!

2-2-14—Jesus paid it all when He died on the cross, and as a result everyone on this planet is offered a full ride scholarship to LIFE.

2-2-14—The only thing we poppin' is the Truth.

2-2-14—When you heard the story about a Hero dying for a villain?! JESUS

2-7-14—Yeah I'm on a mission,
They probably think I'm missin
Some screws but it's those three nails that keep me driven.

2-10-14—People always say count your blessings. Why not count on your blessings. It takes no faith to rejoice in something that already happened. Have faith.

2-11-14—The flesh is weak,
But the spirit is willing.
Spend time with God
And be strong.

2-12-14—Feeling lonely this Valentines week. Did you know that there is a perfectly written out love letter.

2-15-14—Windows down type of day!

2-18-14—I just want to speak on behalf of all the long-boarders out there and say, thank you Jesus for this glorious shredding weather.

2-18-14—If you are driving and have your windows up you

may want to see a doctor; there may be something wrong with you.

2-18-14—The ONLY way we can stand before God on Judgment Day and be righteous is through the PERFECT blood of Jesus.

2-25-14—If you still have a PULSE you still have a PURPOSE.

2-25-14—No place I'd rather be
Than here in your heart
Here in your love.

2-27-14—It's moments like these that keep me going. Don't be afraid to take that initial step to be used of God.   It's so worth it. Thank you, Jesus.

2-28-14—HEY FAM!! Remember Jesus rose from the dead. There ain't NOTHING He can't raise you FROM!!

2-28-14—What kind of King
Chooses a crown
That bleeds and scars
To win my heart.

3-3-14—Why are you believing you are worthless? You have PURPOSE.
God created you didn't He?

3-5-14—Stop worrying about pursuing your future wife and be pursued by God.

3-5-14—Wanna be GREAT? Here's an idea . . .
Why don't you put the E behind the T, end it with ful and be grateful.

3-11-14—Give me 99 problems and 1 Godhead
The result is 100.
You can forget my name
Just remember my Jesus.

3-21-14—God created the world with words alone.
Be careful with what you say
Choose life giving words.
He carried the cross on his shoulders so you could start over.

3-21-14—GOD'S NOT DEAD

3-23-14—What more does He need to do
That He hasn't already done?!
Sent His one and only Son
To die death that we deserved
Make the step
Come home.

3-25-14—So what if they think you the man
That don't mean nothing in the KINGDOM
For a day in your courts is better than a thousand elsewhere. I would rather be a doorkeeper in the house of my God than dwell in the tents of the wicked. Psalm 84:10

4-1-14—NOTHING in this world will EVER satisfy.
I promise you Jesus is the ONLY

Why do the rich consider themselves not rich?
Why the divorce rates?

4-1-14—Life, money, fame are all temporary. Jesus and Heaven are eternal.

4-2-14—There is nothing you can do to make God love you more or less. He loves you for you. Rest in that love.

4-4-14—The only thing you should be doubting is your doubts.

4-11-14—Don't forget to smile today.

4-14-14—Nobody gets remembered tor being comfortable. Make a difference today!

4-16-14—God would rather die to have you than live without you. HE LOVES YOU!

4-18-14—Jesus spent His GOOD FRIDAY getting His back and front torn up for YOU! How will you spend your Good Friday?

4-19-14—Had a great morning with Malcolm Church flying kites and sharing Christ.

4-20-14—Jesus said to her, *"I am the resurrection and the life. Whoever believes in me, though he die, yet shall he live."* John 11:25

He conquered the IMPOSSIBLE so we could be a part of the POSSIBLE.

4-24-14—And I'm His son.
I sing on,
So death can't have that last laugh.
Nothing on this world will satisfy my soul
I'm living for tomorrow today is out of control.

5-2-14—It may not mean much to y'all,
But I know it means the world to my God.

5-22-14—Jesus already likes people that are nothing like Him.
Quit trying to earn it. Just receive it.

6-2-24—Just remember that where you may be in the valley,
God is above on the mountain.

6-6-14—God created all of this for you!
Yes You!
You have purpose!
Don't forget it.

6-17-14—Life isn't fair
Look what WE made Jesus go through.

6-18-14—We don't work for this world.
We work for the next.

6-21-14—"*The heavens declare the Glory of God, the skies proclaim the work of His hands.*" Psalm 19:1

6-22-14—Feeling down on Life? Have Jesus? Remember, the same power that conquered the grave LIVES in YOU!
Man did I need that this morning

6-27-14—To believe that life came from a "Big Bang" is to believe that your life on earth has no purpose that you were an accident.
Let that sink in.

7-21-14—Once you truly experience the Love of God you will NEVER be the same!

Experience it today!

7-22-14—There is nothing like a Your God-centered relationship!

7-23-14—Step aside from the busyness of this world, and you just might find a time worthwhile.

8-30-14—I will praise you the same when no one is around and when the N is on my shirt.
Guide us into battle!

8-31-14—When you go against God's standard
You don't break the standard,
But the standard breaks you.

9-1-14—It feels good so it must be right. Remember every regret started with something good.
Always check your purpose.

Is it heavenly?

9-4-14—The only thing worth boasting;
Please save the air in your lungs.
Everything in life has been given.

9-9-14—There will always be those times in our life where we feel surrounded. Nowhere to go. The enemy.

9-14-14—Not much compares to hearing the GBR chant take over in these away games.

9-20-14—MVP goes to the fans. Y'all were HYPE! #loudest yet #Greatest Fans
Keep us safe Lord for we aren't holding nothing back. #His Glory Alone #GBR

9-23-14—UNL See You at the Pole is tomorrow @7 am @ the flag pole outside east stadium.
Great time to pray with fellow believers.
Who's in?

9-24-14—VIRGINITY is the ONLY thing you can give your spouse that NO ONE else can!
People are made to be test-driven.
Fight for purity today!

9-26-14—Why boast in the created
When you can boast in the CREATOR.

10-4-14—Another week.

Nothing different,
Playing for You alone!
In You we trust.

10-7-14—In every situation ask yourself
What's your motive?
Is it heavenly?

10-21-14—God is ENOUGH.

10-25-14—*Also I heard the voice of the Lord, saying: "Whom shall I send, and who will go for us?" Then I said, "Here am I! Send me."* (Isaiah 6:8)

10-31-14—You are greater than your PAST MISTAKES.

11-1-14—You woke me up this morning,
That's why this day—just like any other day—I live for you.
Don't forget you were wonderfully MADE.

11-13-14—You will never experience the fullness of God until HE is number one in your life.

11-15-14—I love my teammates.

11-23-14—I promise you
Life with Jesus is better
Than life without.

11-24-14—The fact that you are still alive means that God is not done with you yet.

You have purpose

11-28-14—The difference when playing for an audience of 1 is that no matter what the circumstance is you are giving your ALL.
Strengthen us Lord.

12-4-14—It was great meeting @ Coach Riley tonight.
Looking forward to where God leads. Proverbs 3:5-6

12-8-14—No one is born with hate;
It's only learned.

12-10-14—If Heaven ain't a gift,
I ain't getting it.

12-10-14—God is GREATER.
BELIEVE

12-16-14—HE IS Faithful.
Don't EVER FORGET.

12-25-14—JESUS—the only Gift that will truly last.
#Thankful #1 Happy B day

3-1-15—When the Devil reminds you of your past.
Make sure to remind him of his future.

3-4-15—If all you see is what you're not,
You will never see what God intended you to be.

6-2-15—You are a product of your future. Not just your past. Don't let it hold you down.
YOU HAVE PURPOSE!

6-9-15—Had a great time at the Huskers FCA Sand Volley-ball rally last night, #GBR

7-18-15—Knowing the Bible is one thing.
Knowing the Author is another.

7-13-15—Had a solid time kickin it in God's Word w/my Brothers and Sisters! Join us Mondays 7 pm @Destinations Coffee House.

7-21-15—You are not just another number;
You are made in HIS Image.
You have purpose.

3-28-16—Your history doesn't have to dictate your destiny.

3-29-16—Familiarity breeds contentment.

3-30-16—Until God gets ALL of us we will never experience Wholeness IN CHRIST.

3-31-16—There is nothing we can do to be loved more or less by God.

Experience His Love Today!

CHAPTER EIGHT

Direct Ministry

Do not love the world or anything in the world. If anyone loves the world, the love of the Father is not in him. For everything in the world—the cravings of sinful man, the lust of his eyes and the boasting of what he has and does—comes not from the Father but from the world. The world and its desires pass away, but the man who does the will of God lives forever. 1 John 2:15-17

During the early years of his life Graham accomplished most of his efforts for Jesus Christ out of the limelight. He claims that "being in front is not something I enjoy." That thought is undoubtedly an expression of humility, for surely he just doesn't realize how powerfully God touches the hearts and minds of those who hear him. His honest and sincere, off-the-cuff manner of speaking is most appealing.*

In spite of any hesitancy, and in obedience of Christ to *go*, Graham has continued to speak across the state of Nebraska sharing his faith in Jesus with the hope of influencing others to become believers. He is very forthright in his challenge. To a high school assembly in Central City, Nebraska Christian Schools, he asked, "Do you hate someone so much for them to go to hell? Get out of your comfort zone. Be bold!"

In his first missionary journey overseas, in May of his freshman year, he went to South Africa. This was in answer to a challenge from Brett Byford, the Cornhusker team chaplain. In South Africa, Graham fell in love with the ministry to children at Indawo Yethemba Children Village. The children there touched his heart just as the underprivileged kids in Lincoln he had wholeheartedly befriended. He knew he would have to go back there someday.

The following year, in May 2014, at the conclusion of his sophomore year, along with a half-dozen other Husker athletes, Graham made his second missionary journey to serve Native Americans in Washington State. This also was in response to Brett Byford, who set up the trip.

On the way the group stopped in Idaho to enjoy the beautiful scenery gouged out by the Snake River. Being adventurous as always, Graham and Caleb Hawkins, a member of the baseball team, went down to the edge of the fast flowing river. It was quite cold that day—about forty degrees.

Their ambition was to cross the river and climb the other side, but the water was flowing rapidly. They walked along, looking for a crossing spot and were pleased when they found a sandbar where the water was shallow, so they started wading across.

Suddenly, however, there was a deep drop off and they were both plunged into the swirling stream. In desperation, Graham lifted his backpack above his head with his left hand to keep it dry, while struggling to keep afloat with his right arm. Caleb, ahead of him, was having similar problems.

The cold water had a numbing effect on Graham's right arm—and then his leg—until his entire right side was numb and practically useless. Although he was an expert swimmer and had been on swim teams in the past, this was devastatingly different. He was being washed downstream rapidly and sinking beyond relief. He thought death was imminent. In desperation he cried out, "God Help!" Immediately, he heard the response, "Stand up!" He did so, and when he did, his feet touched the solid bottom. He was safe. The water was swirling, but the river at that point was shallow. So, he shouted to Caleb, "Stand up!"

Soaking wet and shivering they walked out of the water to the other side, none the worse for wear, having learned a valuable lesson to trust God in any and every situation.

One of Graham's easiest speaking engagements was for an assembly of grade school kids in Central City, Nebraska Christian Schools. Knowing the attention span of their young students was not very long, the superintendent suggested that they do a question and answer session.

The youngsters were excited to see a Nebraska football player up close and personal. They peppered him with questions about what it was like to be a Cornhusker, how old he was when he started playing football, how good he was, and how long he had been playing. He explained that he played the best he could all the way from age seven. "My uniform was so heavy that I could hardly raise my arm," he explained with a smile. His continual emphasis in his short answers with the kids was to give **glory** to God. "My identity," he told them, "is not in football, but in Jesus."

There were still hands in the air when the superintendent said it was time to close, but Graham had noticed one red-headed little boy who had been anxiously waving his hand to get attention. So he said, "Let's take one more question," and pointed to the boy.

"Can you do a standing back flip?" the boy asked.

Without hesitation, Graham looked around in the crowded space in the front of the room, moved a couple of chairs out of the way, and threw his body head-over-heels into the air in quiet compliance to the request.

The children were delighted and broke into wild applause.

In April, 2017, when speaking to male students at Midland University for their "Restore Conference." Graham built his thoughts around 1 Peter 5:8: *Be self-controlled and alert. Your enemy the devil prowls around like a roaring lion looking for someone to devour.* "It's important," he told them, "to do God-time. For me it's best to begin the day with God, before getting involved with other things—and then having to cry out for help. It's possible, in college life, to get so wrapped up in identities that you leave yourself dry. But, there are ways to combat this; accountability and fellowship are keys to keeping yourself on track spiritually. Who you hang out with is critical to who you become. You, however, are responsible for filling your own cup—even to overflowing for the benefit of others."

Using another analogy he said, "You are like a light bulb. You are useful only when you are connected to your power source. So invest yourself in what has an eternal rate of return. Be bold for Jesus."

In his first ever joint appearance with his dad, Graham was back in Fremont the following week for Good Friday, 2017, to speak for the Fremont Leadership Prayer Breakfast. Dave was up first and told how he came to faith in Christ in 1977. "I was terribly impatient and always on the go. But I learned to slow down and let God lead me. Kim and I were blessed in our home as God gave us four children—girl, boy, girl, boy. We were content; but things can go bad quickly." He then told of the tragic loss of their son Ben, as recounted in chapter two. "It was one of the darkest days of my life," he said. "But I found comfort in 1 Peter 4:1: *Therefore, since Christ suffered in his body, arm yourselves with the same attitude, because he who has suffered in his body is done with sin.*"

Graham focused his talk that morning on how he learned in difficult circumstances at Nebraska to put God first. In that regard he said, "Robbie Trent (FCA) played a huge role in my life. I'm not playing, I'm not enjoying life. I'm a nobody. Why am I here? I want to play football." Trent, however, who is sold totally on playing sports God's way, helped Graham see the beauty of playing circumstance free, as noted in chapter five. That freedom led to the opportunity for Graham to make a huge spiritual difference within the Nebraska football family.

"I want to make God known," Graham told the early morning crowd of more than five hundred. "Who are you living for? Look at the power available to us in Christ. Life in Him is the only thing that lasts and it begins now! We count days that are soon over. Eternity lasts forever."

After the talk, many people came up to congratulate Graham. Among them was Shawn Peterson, a member of the Fremont Chamber of Commerce. "I want to thank you," he said profusely, "for what you did in the last year to help the team hold together in a difficult year. It is so evident to me that God had you there for a purpose."

In regard to his time as a Cornhusker football player, each spring he had to participate in Media Day, where anxious fans could get autographs from the players. Though he always respected the fans and their frequent chant of "Go Big Red," this was different. "I didn't care for it," he said. "It was so twisted, man in a sense worshipping me while the attention should be on God. I struggled on how to point to God in these signature opportunities." He devised a way, however, to get a witness for Christ into his signature—a cross. He elongated the "t" in Nabity, crossed it, and inserted his number 29. (see back cover)

*Author's note: The first time I heard this young man speak was at a Men's Retreat at the SportsBarn in Bennington, Nebraska. I was so impressed by the essence of what he said and how he said it that I told the publisher, who was also present, "I want to write that man's story!" And so I have.

CHAPTER NINE

Then there was Allison

He who finds a wife finds what is good and receives favor from the Lord.
Proverbs 18:22

Throughout his life, even after coming to faith in Jesus Christ, Graham had one major distraction—or was it an attraction—women. We saw previously in chapter two how distraught he was from the breakup with a girl in high school. Even though that led to his salvation in Christ, it indicated this was a problem area in his life. He was always in tune with who the hottest girls around him were. The flesh can be a powerful drag on a young man even though he is seeking to please God in his life, to keep himself pure. This lure is especially accentuated in the all-male society of the locker room talk where the major topic, other than sports, is often about porn sites and messing with the hottest chicks.

During his years as a Husker, occasionally Graham would have to find a last minute place to bunk for the night when his college roommate would text him, "Stay away from the room tonight. I have a girl coming."

Through FCA and the Navigator organization on campus—and of course classes—Graham had a lot of female friends, but no one girlfriend. He was waiting for the "right" woman. Then, at the end of the fall of his redshirt sophomore year on a ski trip with the Navigators at Colorado Springs, he caught a glimpse of her, and she surely caught his attention.

Before Graham left on the ski trip he had cancelled one of his classes for business economics for the next semester. However, when he found out while on this ski trip that this special girl, Allison Key, was taking the class, he quickly re-enrolled when he got back to Lincoln. They became study partners and often used the sky boxes to do their studying, high above Memorial Stadium.

Her sorority sisters were impressed that she was friends with a football player, but that wasn't Allison's attraction. "Above everything else, what I liked most about him," she said, "was his love for Jesus."

Incredibly their paths had come close to crossing twice before. Before the Keys moved to Lincoln, they and the Nabity's lived in the same neighborhood. Graham and Allison attended the same elementary school, living less than a mile apart until the Keys later moved to Lincoln. In Lincoln, Allison and her family attended the First Evangelical Free Church, where she came to faith in Christ. For high school she went to Lincoln East; but when Graham, a member of the Cornhusker Football Team went to speak to the East FCA Huddle, she wasn't there—she was at home sick. Before that, she had never missed an FCA huddle meeting. Isn't it funny how God works.

The summer after Graham's redshirt sophomore year, his mind and heart were made up and he decided to approach Allison's dad Greg Key and ask "may I date your daughter?"

There was no hesitancy on Greg Key's part, as he gave two valuable pieces of advice, "My daughter wants to be pursued. Respect her!"

For their first official date, Graham sent her a note with instructions for a miniature scavenger hunt, where he would be waiting at the conclusion with flowers and a hammock set with tiki torches and all the works. The plan then was to go for ice cream, but there his finely laid plan fell apart; he had only a credit card—she paid for the treat with cash.

"My attraction to her was a mixture of a lot of things," Graham said. "Her intense desire for the Lord, and watching her serve alongside me with kids at the Mission and with the youth at Christ's Place Church were special.

"She was the one person I always wanted to be around. We were truly best friends. She is beautiful and elegant, yet she can keep up with my crazy adventures, like jumping off the bridge into lakes and rivers.

"She has a joy that is contagious and warms up the room. She loves kids, and is the woman I would love to be the mother of my children."

After graduating from UNL, Allison started to work immediately for Lifetime Fitness in Omaha. Graham, however, had an adventure in mind—a trip to South Africa—to introduce his-bride-to-be with a ministry that is close to his heart, the South Africa Children's Resiliency Project. Fortunately he didn't try to surprise her with last minute tickets [she needed a passport and was having multiple interviews]. Her boss at Lifetime Fitness was very understanding of the situation. After working for just a month, she was free to go for three weeks.

Just as Graham had previously, she too loved the experience. She threw herself into the maintenance work on the facility, and picking up kids from the various schools they attended, and helping them with their homework, and playing with them. "Adventure," Allison said, "is not outside. It's within me."

It was through these events Graham and Allison drew close to each other and deepened their walk with Christ. Their love for each other grew first through being good friends, then serving the Lord in children's ministry together.

*To the only wise God be **glory** forever through Jesus Christ! Amen,* Romans 16:27

There is nothing truly unique or special about Graham Nabity. He is so much like millions of others who love and follow the Lord Jesus Christ. What makes his story worth telling is that he never allowed what happened in his life—good or bad—to determine who he was as a man of God. Once he came into a personal relationship with God through faith in Christ Jesus as a teenager, he strove continually to give all honor and **glory** to God.

He accepted the solemn words of his Savior as expressed in Luke 17:10: *So you also, when you have done everything you were told to do, should say, "We are unworthy servants, we have only done our duty."*

It is true that Graham was good as a University of Nebraska football player, but not exceptional. He was also good within his family as a son and brother and grandson and uncle, but not exceptionally so. He was seen good as a friend to all who knew him, kind, thoughtful and considerate. In that regard perhaps he was more exceptional than most. For this very reason he stands as an example to everyone who hears of him, because he made the most of that with which God entrusted him. We should do the same.

Many times we make decisions and walk through life's trials in the obvious direction, the logical direction, which can end up being the wrong direction. God has a vantage point none of us have. He knows the consequences of decisions we will make. He can see how things will turn out. He also knows what is best for us. He has given us His Holy Spirit to be our Counselor and Guide to help us gain peace and confidence to walk paths that just don't seem logical.

For Graham, playing at Nebraska didn't seem logical to his dad. Dave wanted him to go someplace where he could have fun playing football. He wanted his son to have coaches who respected and appreciated Graham's talents and would work to help him excel as a player. Dave's experience had taught him that his son should go where he would get the most encouragement to thrive. Graham, on the other hand, only wanted to hear from God and was not willing to make the "logical" decision to transfer to another school.

Had he taken matters in his own hands and transferred, there are a whole host of things that could have gone wrong. As it turned out, Graham fulfilled God's call on his life with regard to being on a football team and representing Christ to his coaches, fellow players, and fans. He was in the right place, at the right time, to minister to those who were hurting from the loss of Sam Foltz.

In honoring God, it was never about football for Graham. It was about serving Christ on a team that needed spiritual leadership during some very trying times. Graham's example of waiting on the Lord and not acting on fleshly logic, allowed him to step into God's plan.

God has a strategic plan for each of us. It is a good design, having eternal consequences along the way. Are you willing to allow God to guide you? Are you willing to wait on Him and only move toward a destination God is directing you? Staying planted where you are until God opens another door

is an important insight to be gained from Graham's experience of playing football at the University of Nebraska.

There are at least three lessons that can be learned from
Graham's story.

The most important is to learn the exceptional joy of
knowing the presence of God Almighty. Graham had struggled through the first fifteen years of his life, making himself
and others around him miserable by constantly seeking what
was to his satisfaction. When things didn't go his way he was
"Grumpy Graham." That began to change, however, when he
was all alone in his bedroom one night, pouring out his heart
to God. And God was gracious—as He always is to anyone
who seeks Him with all his heart. There was no flash of light
that night, no thunder. Rather there was the calming assurance of a Holy Presence—the Shekinah* **glory** of God came
upon him in a gentle fashion.

With that experience, Graham learned to trust in the
peace and confidence that God alone can give. And, in that
regard, once again, Graham is not exceptional. God does not
show partiality but will respond to anyone who calls on Him
in faith.

A second invaluable lesson is this. When anyone comes
into that qualitative relationship with God through Jesus
Christ there is a major change of attitude.

The Apostle Paul describes it best in Philippians 2:1-5: *If
you have any encouragement from being united with Christ, if any
comfort from his love, if any fellowship with the Spirit, if any ten-
derness and compassion, then make my joy complete by being like-
minded, having the same love, being one in spirit and purpose. Do
nothing out of selfish ambition or vain conceit, but in humility consider others better than yourselves. Each of you should look not only*

to your own interests, but also to the interest of others. Your attitude
should be the same as that of Jesus Christ.

That is a radical transformation of life, in contrast to the
"me first" society of the world. It wipes away conflict by
putting the needs and wants of others ahead of your own.
Such an attitude is called humility. Paul continues in that portion of Scripture to detail how greatly Jesus humbled himself
for the sake of all mankind—by death on the cross.

An athletic field is a perfect place to put this concept of
humility into action. You owe it to your opponent to perform
at your very best in order for him/her to have the best possible test of his/her endeavor. No true athlete wants you to
rollover and let them win. That would be both prideful and
insulting.

Graham exhibited that desire to serve others in his constant effort to share the message of Jesus to his teammates
and coaches, with underprivileged kids, and anyone out there
on the internet. However, as seen in the previous pages, it was
not easy to stay the course. It would have been nice to have
been recognized for all the sweat and bumps and bruises.
That, though, is the way of life for most people. There is no
fanfare for simply enduring. Take the hardworking farmer for
example; he is an unsung hero—even to those who eat the
fruit of his labors, but, what would life be like without him?

Everyone would like to hear an atta-ta-boy now and then.
Unfortunately, they don't come often enough.

So the third lesson of living circumstance free is that it is
necessary for anyone who wants to navigate this wide world
successfully. What Graham and other athletes learned about
playing for an audience of one is also a necessary guideline for
a nine-to-five office worker: *And whatever you do, whether in*

word or deed, do it all in the name of the Lord Jesus Christ, giving thanks to God the Father through him. Colossians 3:17. *Whatever* means whatever. It does not apply just to football players.

Graham Nabity now has an opportunity to test that out in "the real world." Presently he is one of those nine-to-five guys, marketing commercial real estate through the GBRE|Mega firm in Omaha. After work he has the joy of going home to face a loving wife.

Yes!

He and Allison were united in wedded bliss on June 17, 2017 in front of more than four hundred guests. Typical of the two of them, who love all of their Father's creation, they chose an outdoor setting on a farm outside of Roca, Nebraska for the nuptials. And, so as not to exclude anyone, they had to have fifteen attendants.

For their honeymoon, it was all about adventure! They found a great getaway spot, complete with a "Tiki Hut" bungalow (over the water) in Panama, with a crystal clear view of the Caribbean.

As they returned back to the real world after their getaway, they took to heart the encouraging words Moses gave to the Israelites in Deuteronomy 31:8: *The Lord himself goes before you and will be with you; he will never leave you nor forsake you. Do not be afraid; do not be discouraged.*

---

*Shekinah is the Hebrew word to express the manifestation of God's presence on earth.

Arthur L. Lindsay has been active as a public speaker, having spoken in ten countries on four continents. He has three living children: Tedrin Blair, Timothy Arthur, Linda Mae, and a deceased son, Robert Colin.

Art has been a resident of Lincoln, Nebraska since 1988. Prior to that, he spent 16 years of missionary service in Rome, Italy. Though he has many varied interests, his primary focus is his own personal relationship with God through Jesus Christ. Therefore, he consistently studies and memorizes the Word of God. He employs that knowledge with men in one-on-one discipleship training. Additionally, he has been involved in prison ministry for nearly sixty years.

He is the author of thirteen previous books, five of which are biographies—I Can, Coach Ron Brown's Search for Success—Not Even a Thread: When a rapist repents . . . God—One Final Pass, the Brook Berringer Story—I Can 2—and One Final Pass, 15 Years Later. There have been five histories—*It Takes a Home: commemorating 90 years of service of People's City Mission—Most Unusual Packages, the story of Bethphage—Influence, a history of the Nebraska Fellowship of Christian Athletes—A Tree Grows in Lincoln, a history of Christ temple Church—* and *The Diary, a World War Two hero story. Art has also written one novel—Three Wings Against the Monkey—*and two books on ethics for the insurance industry—*Don't Punt—*and—*Cover All the Bases.*